The Nottingham Knight Writer

A Student Anthology

A collection of stories and poems written by the students of Nottingham Elementary School

2008-2009

Self-Published
Arlington, Virginia

Published in the United States of America
By Nottingham Elementary School
5900 Little Falls Road
Arlington, VA 22207
www.apsva.us/nottingham

Copyright © 2009 by the students of Nottingham Elementary School (2008-2009)

All rights reserved. No part of this publication my be reproduced, stored in a retrieval system, or transmitted in any form or by any means, electronic, mechanical, photocopying, recording, or otherwise, without the prior permission of the publisher.

ISBN-13: 978-0-615-29207-6 (paperback)
ISBN-10: 06152920707 (paperback)

Nottingham Elementary, 2009 -

Cover design: Mary Jane Hickey, Ink Graphics, Arlington, VA
Cover photo by: Lee Morales

This book was printed in the United States by Todd Allan Printing
5760 Sunnyside Avenue
Beltsville, MD 20705
Www.toddallan.com

To young writers everywhere,
May these stories and poems inspire you to share your writing with others.

"Words are the key to the heart" ~ Anonymous

Providing a medium for children to share their words with an authentic audience makes writing a truly meaningful experience. The Knight Writer Exemplary Project is designed to invite children at all grade levels to share their thoughts, ideas and inspiration with others. What better format to achieve this goal than through the publishing of a real book?! It has been a truly rewarding experience to see all of the students at Nottingham Elementary School evolve and grow as writers as they prepared their pieces for the Knight Writer book. From the newest kindergarten learner to the budding fifth grade poet, all of our students did a phenomenal job working their way through the writing process to produce the pieces included in this book. Hats off to them and to all of their teachers who supported the process along the way!

Mary Beth Pelosky, Principal
Beth Smith, Exemplary Project Coordinator

Junior Editors

Kate Burkholder
Rachel Cohen
Sofia Cohen
Bennett Crow
Gabrielle Economos
Kelly Emson
Abby England
Reiss Gidner
Megan Grieco
Maddie McNamee
Bryn O'Neil
Nicholas Saunders
Joanna Schroeder
Katie Smith
Ellie Styles
Reilly Tickle
Isabel Zavada
Jack Zellum

Thank You!

A heartfelt, "Thank you!" to the Nottingham PTA for their financial support of the printing of this book. Without them, none of this would be possible! Thanks also to all of the parent volunteers who helped both in the classroom and with the many rounds of edits needed to make this book truly phenomenal!

Special thanks to Mary Jane Hickey, Nottingham parent and owner of Ink Graphics, for the her help in designing the cover of this book and new Nottingham Knight Writer logo!

Many thanks to the many parent volunteers who helped in so many ways to make this book possible. From conferencing with students to proofreading, it would not have been possible without your help!

Purpose and Vision

The Nottingham Knight Writer Exemplary Project is a unique writing program supported by the Arlington Public Schools and the Nottingham PTA. The goal of the project is to help all students experience the entire writing process from drafting to publishing. By exploring different genres, students at different grade levels are provided with a unique opportunity to share their knowledge on many different topics with their readers. Through the Knight Writer Exemplary Project, students are invited to share their writing with an authentic, diverse audience that includes their school, family and community.

Table of Contents

KINDERGARTEN: My Wonderful World … Traveling

Mrs. Cooper's Koalas……………………………………………	pp. 6-15
Mr. Galloway's Bunnies……………………………………….	pp. 16-27
Ms. Helmstreet's Hippos………………………………………	pp. 28-37
Mrs. Howards's Warthogs…………………………………….	pp. 38-47
Mrs. Toner's Pooh Bears………………………………………	pp. 48-59

FIRST GRADE: My Wonderful World

Ms. Gassman's Lovebugs…………………………………….	pp. 60-69
Mrs. Jensen's Jolly Rogers…………………………………..	pp. 70-79
Ms. Kepchar's Kangaroos…………………………………….	pp. 80-89
Mrs. Lee's Elephants………………………………………….	pp. 90-99

SECOND GRADE: Let's Discover … Animals

Mr. Flood's Falcons ………………………………………….. .	pp. 100-111
Mr. Katoen's Tigers…………………………………………. .	pp. 112-123
Mrs. Stegall's Seagulls……………………………………….	pp. 124-135
Mrs. Way's Wise Owls………………………………………. .	pp. 136-147

THIRD GRADE: My Incredible Imagination … Inventions

Mrs. Gorham/Lamb's Hall of Famers…………………………….	pp. 148-157
Mr. Knott's Bulldogs…………………………………………..	pp. 158-167
Ms. Schaefer's Scholars………………………………………	pp. 168-177
Mrs. Stewart's Superstars…………………………………….	pp. 178-187

FOURTH GRADE: Let's Discover … Our World

Ms. Barber's Barbershop………………………………………	pp. 188-199
Mrs. Costa's Cardinals……………………………………….	pp. 200-211
Ms. Matthews' Mariners………………………………………	pp. 212-225

FIFTH GRADE: My Incredible Imagination

Ms. Ashley's Smarties……………………………………….	pp. 226-235
Mrs. Jones' Gems…………………………………………….	pp. 236-247
Mr. Young's Einsteins………………………………………..	pp. 248-257

My Wonderful World ... Traveling

Going to Amsterdam
By Alexandra P.

Theresa, Mom, Dad and I went to Amsterdam in winter. We took a taxi and an airplane. We did our puzzle books. We went there because my dad had a meeting and to see a castle and we went inside the castle. We also saw a fancy house. We had croissants every day.

We went to a science museum. There was a bubble thing. In the canals, they had ducks. My sister had to sleep on the floor every night. I had a fun time.

To the Beach
By Anna S.

Sam, Nick, Dad, Mom and I took a minivan. We went to the Outer Banks in North Carolina because we wanted to swim. We went in the summer!

In the car my baby brother threw his Cheerios. They were in the front seat and back seat. Then, when we got there, all of the Cheerios fell out of the car. We giggled a lot when we saw the Cheerios on the ground.

I played in the ocean! We felt excited about our trip!

By Mrs. Cooper's Koalas

K

My Texas Trip
By Colin O.

Ryan, Sabrina, Daddy, Mommy and I went to Texas in summer time. We went in a silver minivan. I had a snack and we watched a movie.

I went to see my cousins. We threw rocks over a cliff. When we were trying to catch a frog, my cousin caught the frog. He put the frog on the table, but he got away. I had a good time!

Disney World and SeaWorld
By Cooper C.

I went to Disney World and SeaWorld in March. Mom, Anne Marie, Granddaddy, Nini and I rode in Mom's car to the airport. We rode on the airplane to Orlando, Florida. We wanted to have fun.

We saw an orca show. At the show, Shamu splashed me and Granddaddy. It was cold. We laughed! I have three stuffed Shamus.

We also went to a big castle. There were princesses surrounding it. I wish I could go back with my mom and my dad.

My Wonderful World ... Traveling

Disneyland
By Emma F.

Mom, Dad, Morgan and I are going to Disneyland in April. We will ride in our car to the airport. We will get on the airplane. We will go to the Bippity Boppity Boutique, ride rides, and swim in the pool. My sister and I are going to get our nails done at the boutique. We will get our hair done with glitter. We will have an awesome time!

Boston
By Evangeline M.

Dad, Mom, Jack and I went to Boston. We drove in our van. We watched a movie. We were going to visit my mom's family. We went to the movies and we saw "Bolt." We stayed at my mom's sister's house. They have a pool, but we didn't go in it because it was too cold. We went to our cousin's house and we played Wii Fit. We had a great time!

By Mrs. Cooper's Koalas

K

My Awesome Trip to Ohio
By Jack F.

My mom and dad and my sisters and I went to Ohio last year in the summer. I got there by minivan. I went there to visit my grandma and granddad.

My grandparents took care of me while my mom and dad were gone. We went swimming. We saw my cousins, and I went to the zoo with my cousins. I saw an ostrich at the zoo and elephants. I think I saw wild birds. I had a fantastic time!

The Golf Award Trip
By Jack P.

Mom, Dad, G-Dad, Shar-Shar and I went to Houston, Texas for G-Dad's award. We got there in a car and an airplane.

I went to a super fun waterpark aquarium. I saw an electric eel. I also saw a moray eel and piranhas. I also saw sharks. They are not the kind of sharks you think of, like great white sharks or tiger sharks. I want to go there a million times more!

My Wonderful World ... Traveling

Going to New Zealand
By James S.

I took three planes to New Zealand to see my grandma and grandpa. Lucille, my mom, my dad, my grandma, and I all went. I saw a huge chicken. The chicken was almost eight feet long. It lived on my uncle's farm. I am happy that I am going this year again!

The Mexico Story
By Julia J.

Jordan, Mom, Dad, and I and three other families are going to Mexico for Easter. We are taking an airplane. We will sleep in princess beds. We will swim and play in the ocean. We are going to play in the sand and live in sheds. We have a pool. It is in the middle of the huts. I am excited about going to Mexico!

By Mrs. Cooper's Koalas

K

Riding Planes
By Kai P.

Allyssa, Mommy, Daddy and I came to the U.S.A. in March. We came from Adelaide. We took lots of airplanes. We came here to see San Francisco. We looked around. Then, we took two planes to get here. It is good to be in Washington!

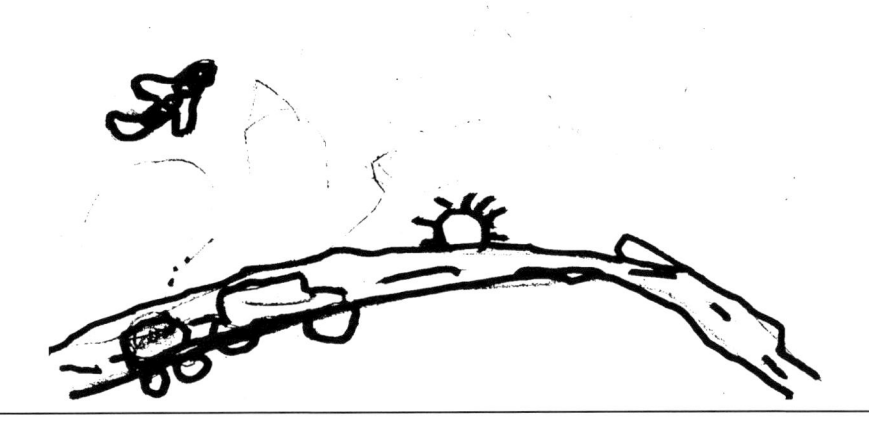

My Family Goes to the Beach
By Lauren M.

Puppy, Daddy, Mommy and I are going to the beach in April. I am riding in my car with my mom and dad to the beach. I am going to swim. I am going to build a big, gigantic sandcastle. I will decorate it with seashells. I will go inside it. It will make me feel tired to make it. The beach is fantastic!

My Wonderful World ... Traveling

New York
By Mary Bernadette B.

My mom and dad and I went to New York last summer. We rode in a car. We went to see my cousins. Rose is four and Thomas is one. We had so much fun! We had fun on the slide and on the swing. I want to go back to see my cousins again.

The Trip to See Nana and Tom
By Morgan D.

Dog, Mom, Dad, Dane and I went to Michigan in the summer. We rode in a car in one day to see Nana and Tom. We played games.
It was fun there. She has a bowling set. We played the bowling game. It was fun. We set it up and we played. We rolled the ball. It was a good trip!

By Mrs. Cooper's Koalas

Niko Goes to Pennsylvania
By Niko E.

Dad, Mom, my sister, Moo and I went to Pennsylvania. We drove a car. When were driving, we watched a movie. When we got there, we went to Hershey Park. We rode on a ride and we saw cows that sang. It was great! The cows had collars. They gave me chocolate.

I saw a Hershey dude. He was funny. I liked him. I really liked him. Then when I left, I got chocolate kisses. They tasted sweet. I wish I could have another chocolate kiss. Boy, they were good! I wish I could have one hundred of them, but I would be sick.

I was joyous about my trip!

Seeing the Gigantic Moth
By Noah P.

Mommy, Daddy, Ben and I went to Taiwan last, last, last year. We rode on a 747. It took one night. We got there three years ago.

We saw a gigantic moth that landed on Dad's foot. It was in the mountains. We did one hundred trips to the mountains. This was my favorite trip because we saw the gigantic moth.

My Wonderful World ... Traveling

The New York Fun
By Simon P.

Gwen and Dad and Mom and I went to New York. We rode in my car to see my grandpa and my grandma. We ate veggies and pudding.
I snorkeled. I went fishing. I caught eight fish. I sat on a bench to fish. I caught sailfish. It was sunny. I went on a boat then. It was so fun!

California for Easter
By Thor K.

Thor, Mom, Dad, Ben and Thomas are going to California for Easter. We are taking our car to the airport. We will take our plane. We will meet my cousins! I will have a great time!
We are going to San Francisco. I hope we get to ride the cable cars. I can't wait!

By Mrs. Cooper's Koalas

K

When I Went to Washington, D.C.
By Tony W.

My dad, my brother, and my sister and I went to Washington, D. C. We drove in a car. We saw the Washington Monument. I was happy. I saw the Lincoln Memorial. I went up the stairs to see the statue of Abraham Lincoln. I think this trip was fun!

My Trip
By Maddie H.

In November, Becca, Mommy, Daddy and I went to Disney World in Florida. We flew in a plane. My suitcase was purple. Short-sleeved shirts and sandals were in my suitcase. I did not bring my school shoes because they are hot. I brought my Minnie Mouse dress. I brought my doll, Molly, too. She had a Mickey Mouse shirt.

At the airport, we picked a blue car. I sat in a car seat and Daddy drove to our condo. Becca and I shared a room. It had two beds and a TV. Becca, Molly and I got to watch the Disney Channel in bed. Molly slept with me. We both wore short-sleeved pajamas. Mine were Tinkerbell.

At Disney World, I bought a Mickey Mouse for my Crocs. I brought my yellow bikini and my flowered towel. I swam in two pools. We went on the "It's a Small World" ride. Becca and I saw Mickey and Minnie Mouse. They signed a book for us. Molly had to stay at our condo.

We made our own food. I got to make my own lunch. I ate peanut butter sandwiches. I brought my LL Bean lunchbox and carried it in my backpack. We ate lunch at a table in Disney World. One day, we ate at our condo because it was raining. When our trip was over, we all flew home.

My Wonderful World ... Traveling

The Trip to Rhode Island
By Kate L.

Me, Daddy, Sophie and Mom went to Rhode Island. First, we drove our car to the airport. Then I remember feeling hungry and excited. My uncle picked us up and we went to my Nana's house. After that, I played with my American Girl dolls with my cousins. It was awesome!

Me and Adam
By Wyatt B.

Me and my dad are going to Adam's house to play football. We are going in a car on spring break. Adam is a great cousin and we are going to have an awesome time together!

By Mr. Galloway's Bunnies K

The Trip to Florida
By Catherine D.

Me, Meghan, Mom and my Dad went to Florida a long time ago to have fun. We drove to the airport and parked in the parking lot. We then got on the plane. We flew to Florida and then we got off the plane. My grandparents picked us up in their car and we drove to their house. We had a great time at my grandparent's house! We swam in the swimming pool. It was really hot in Florida.

Going to Panama
By Liam A.

Me, Mom, Dad, Gavin and Declan are going to Panama for spring break. We are taking a taxi on the highway to Dulles Airport. At the airport, you get to watch the planes take off while you wait. When we land in Panama, the taxi will take us to our hotel. I can't wait to go to the rainforest! I am going to ride down the zipline. I think it will be lots of fun!

My Wonderful World ... Traveling

Going to My Cousin's House
By Patrick C.

Me, Conor, Kelly, Dad and Mom went to New Jersey on the 26th of November. We took a taxi to the airport. We got on a plane. We went to visit our relatives. They picked us up from the airport and drove us to their house. We went to the pool and I went off the diving board. I was not scared. It was a lot of fun! Aunt Kathy, Ryan, Megan and Tyler watched us have fun.

Trip to West Virginia
By Sophia S.

Me, Mommy, Daddy and Lucy are going to West Virginia in April. We are driving there in our car. It will take four hours to get there. We are going to my uncle and aunt's house. We will be celebrating my birthday. When we get there, we will have a lot of fun. I hope to play with my cousins that will be visiting also. They live in Pennsylvania. We will be there for the Easter weekend.

By Mr. Galloway's Bunnies

K

When I Went to the Beach
By Henry H.

Me, Brendan, Mom, Dad and Gus went on a trip to South Carolina on August 8, 2008. We drove there in our car. It took a long time to get there. We went there to visit the beach. We went to play and have fun! We stayed in a hotel that was right on the beach. We could walk to the ocean. When I was swimming in the ocean, I got knocked over by a small wave! I fell down and hit the sand. I think I hurt my knee when I fell. We stayed at the beach for a long time. We then drove back home on the highway.

My Wonderful World ... Traveling

Trip to Disney
By Joey N.

Mom, Dad, Justin, Matthew and I went to have fun last summer in Disney World. We took a bluish-greenish car to the airport. We went on an airplane. We had fun and we rode on rides. My favorite ride was Pirates of the Caribbean because it was dark. I liked Disney World because it was fun.

Florida
By Gavin P.

Mommy, Keely and I went to Disney World. We went in January 2008. Daddy drove us to the airport and we took a plane to Florida. I went to the beach and saw big fish. It was really hot in Florida, but the ocean water was cool! We stayed there for five days. We then took an airplane back home. I had a fun time!

By Mr. Galloway's Bunnies

K

Flying to Florida
By Ben I.

Jack, Dad, Mom and I are going to Florida. We will take a taxi to the airport. Then we will take a JetBlue plane. I will watch a movie while we fly to the Florida airport. Somebody will pick us up and they will take us to their house. They are our friends. We will sleep there for one week. We will go swimming at the pool. I will feed the fish at the dock. I will go golfing with my dad. I will have dinner next to the swimming pool.

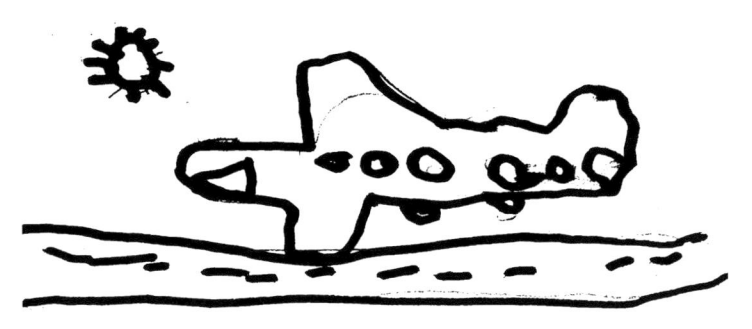

Our Florida Trip
By Reilly M.

Mommy, Daddy, Brendan and I went to Florida in 2008. We drove there in a blue car. It took until nighttime. We went because I like going there. I swam in the pool. It was really warm. I could touch the bottom of eight feet. I stayed in a really big hotel. It had a bedroom and a kitchen. I had a great time and it was fun to stay in a hotel!

My Wonderful World ... Traveling

Flying to London
By Declan D.

Me, Mommy, Dad, Bridget and Grammy are going to London for spring break. We will take Mommy's grey car to the airport. We will get on a giant airplane. We will eat breakfast and dinner on the plane. I will draw while I fly on the plane. We are going to visit Auntie Babs. I will have an egg hunt in Auntie Babs' room with Bridget. I know I will find the most eggs. A little bit later, Auntie Babs will have another egg hunt with other kids in the backyard. It will be a really fun trip!

Australia
By Avery P.

We went for a trip. Me, Mom, Dad, Dash and Graham went to Australia. We went on a big, white airplane. I drew a picture of a unicorn while I rode on the airplane. I ate an apple and I drank some water. We went for vacation. We played at the pool. We played at the hotel. I had my birthday party and we went to the swimming pool again. We went back to the hotel room and changed into dry clothes and then we went back home.

By Mr. Galloway's Bunnies

K

I'm Going to Alaska
By Jack E.

Mom, Dad, Olivia and I are going to Alaska during summer break. We will drive to the airport in our silver car and then get on an airplane. We are going because my cousins are moving there. We will go sightseeing. We might see big, grey mountains with snow on top. We might feel cold wind. I am happy we are going there.

Christmas in Canada
By Emily C.

Me, Ryan, Mommy and Daddy went to Montreal in December. We rode a car to Montreal and we went to Grandma and Puppa's house to have Christmas. I played in the snow and I helped Grandma put on the Christmas tree decorations. I had a lot of fun.

My Wonderful World ... Traveling

Driving to Florida
By Amelia H.

Mom, Dad, Emma, Anna, Isabelle and I went to Florida a while ago. We drove in our white SUV. It took two days to get there. We finally got to the beach. We played on the sand. When I played in the ocean, the waves kept knocking me down. I had a fun time there because I found a live crab on the beach. We watched it crawl on the sand. I liked the beach.

Car Ride to Corolla
By Madeline L.

My mom, dad, Kate and Zoey, our dog, and I are going to the beach. We are going to take a car. After the car ride, we will unpack our bags. We are going in April. We are going to play on the beach.

By Mr. Galloway's Bunnies

K

Summer Time
By Sam H.

Me, Mom, Dad, Elijah and Ben are going to Colorado on June 29th. We are going to drive and go there for my birthday. We will have fun at Grandpa and Grandma's house. Two of my uncles live there, too. I would like to go to the beach.

Flying to Florida
By Mary C.

Emily, Christian, Mommy, Daddy and I are going to Florida before Easter. We will ride in a taxi to the airport and then take a plane to Florida. We are going to play at the beach and go to Disney World. It will be a lot of fun.

2009 © Nottingham Elementary School

My Wonderful World ... Traveling

My Trip to New Jersey
By Mackenzie K.

Me, Mommy, Daddy, Sean and Westen are going to New Jersey in April for Easter. We are driving in my mom's van. When we get there, we will unpack our black suitcases. When we get there, we will have lunch. We will see our cousins.

By Mr. Galloway's Bunnies

My Trip Puerto Rico
By Olivia B.

One time, me, Mommy, Daddy and Hayden went to Puerto Rico in January 2009! We got to the airport by taxi and got to Puerto Rico by a big plane. We went to get out of the cold and to have fun with my family! I lost a tooth and got money!!! We went swimming in the pool. We stayed in a hotel and our car smelled bad. We went out to eat and saw two cats. They were eating off people's plates and I petted them. Hayden did, too. We took a boat to the private island. We went swimming in the warm, blue water. I loved my trip!

My Wonderful World ... Traveling

My Favorite Trip
By Caleb M.

Me, Daddy, Mom and my brother Jonah took a car and an airplane. We went to Chicago last year to see my uncle and aunt. We all went to a restaurant. There was spaghetti and meatballs. It was great! I loved it. My brother loves spaghetti and meatballs. Our room was cozy. I loved my room. There are beds and a wonderful view. It was busy. I saw a skyscraper. It was awesome. Do you like skyscrapers? We took a van to get back to the airport. They came to our hotel. We had pancakes and a drink. The trip was great! We loved it. Do you want to go there?

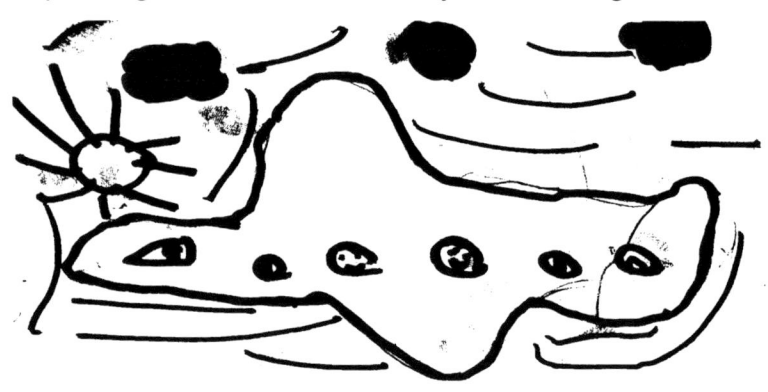

The Car Trip
By Lauren S.

I went to Nonny and Granddad's house. I took a car because my Mommy and Daddy are going on a trip. I had fun. I got a Lite Brite. I also got a calendar and on every page there was a hidden picture. I went to an indoor playground place. It was fun! Would you like to go there? When we got back, we had pizza and we watched TV. I had fun!

By Ms. Hemstreet's Hippos

K

My Trip to Atlanta
By Heidi H.

Me and Dad and Mom and James went to Atlanta. We took a plane and a car. It was fun riding in a plane. We went when I was three years old. We went in November. I had never been in the airport. It was fun inside it! It was fun looking at the planes. My uncle invited us to a Thanksgiving party. I stayed at my uncle's house for three nights and days. We went to the aquarium one day. We saw whale sharks and beluga whales, too. It was fun at the aquarium. I liked it.

We Went to Mexico
By Anthony G.

Me and Matey, Sammy, Zachy, Jo, Mark, Yiayla, Papou, Aunt Arlene and Uncle Pete went to Mexico. We had a big hotel near the pool. We went to the pool. It was very hot. We had to go to the restaurant every night because there was no food in the hotel. We had a great time. Every night I was very hungry. It was exciting.

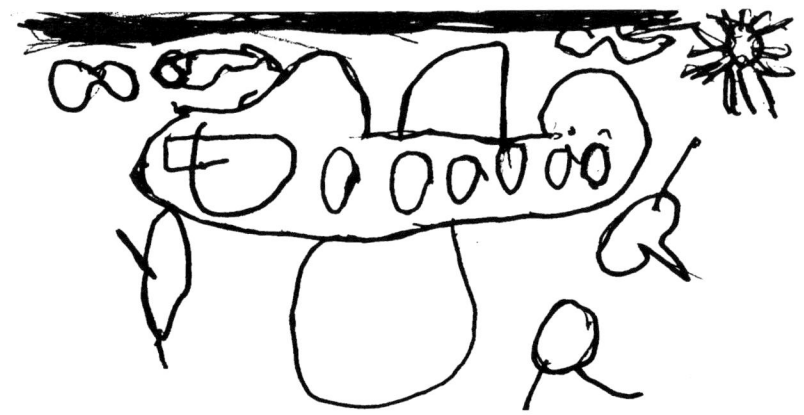

My Wonderful World ... Traveling

Going to New York City
By Sloane S.

Last November, Mom, me, Katie, Allie and Mimi went to New York. First, we took a car. Then we walked. Then we took a cab. My mom wanted me to see the Rockettes. I got to eat popcorn. It was fun! I got to ride on a train. It was fun, too! Allie and I played with our Leapsters.

My Trip to Florida
By Sophie Y.

This March, my mom, my dad and my sisters (Emma and Natalie) and me are going to Florida. We will go in a taxi. Then we will go on an airplane. I like that it goes really fast. We go so we can go on the rides at Disney World. I like Disney World because it has a lot of things to do. It has a spooky ride. I like to go on the merry-go-round. We will go on a boat to Disney World. It will be fun. My grammy is coming for one day. My grammy is coming for one day because my dad and mom are going out to dinner. My dad and my mom are going to Pie Tanza.

By Ms. Hemstreet's Hippos

K

Going to Mexico
By Fiona S.

Last April, Mom, Dad, Bryan and I went to Mexico. We took a plane. We went swimming in a pool. We had an airplane float. Me and Bryan rode on it in the water! We went to the beach and played in the water. There were hammocks! We went for a walk. We took an airplane home. It was fun!

My Trip to DC
By Evan F.

I went with my mom and dad and Ben to DC. We got there by a train and we walked. We went to DC on Tuesday. We went to go see the museum. It looked good at DC. I saw a truck, train and a spaceship. We ate there. I ate chicken nuggets and French fries. It was fun!

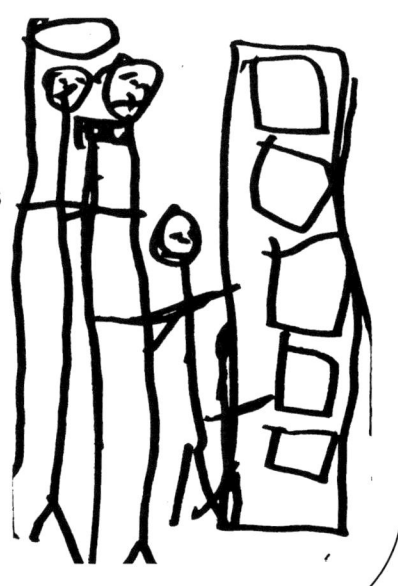

My Wonderful World ... Traveling

I Am Going to Puerto Rico
By Daisy B.

I am going to Puerto Rico with my mom, dad, my brother, my Granpy and of course, my dolls. It will take two days to get there and it will take two days to get back. But it will be fun. I hope my dog can go because I love her. I am going to ride on an plane. I can't wait. It will be fun. We are going there in three months.

The Trip to Mexico
By Kaitlyn P.

Last year, Mom, Dad, me, Mimi and Papa went to Mexico on a plane. I went to the kid's club. The teachers were nice. Iguanas lived under the clubhouse. In Mexico, we took a train. On the train, I got a badge that said, "Good sport" for buckling my seatbelt. The badge was gold. It was very fun. The next day, we went to the pool and I got my hair braided. It was fun. The next day, we went home. We took a van to get to the airport.

By Ms. Hemstreet's Hippos K

My Trip to Disneyland
By John B.

I went on a trip with part of my family. I went with my dad and my sister and other people in my family. We went to Disneyland. We went last year. We went on a roller coaster. It was fun. At the hotel, we went to a place for breakfast, lunch and dinner. The Disney stars came out. We had to take an airplane to get home.

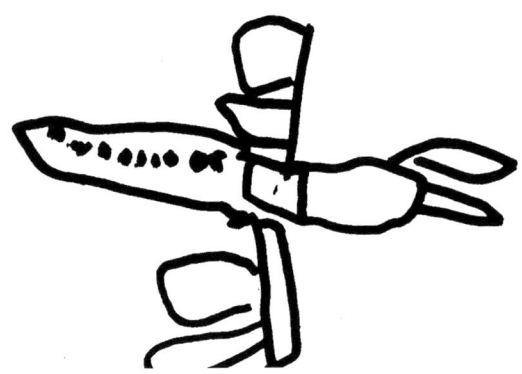

The Trip
By Russ P.

I went with Dad and Mom on a plane to Florida. We went in March to see the shuttle launch. My mom works for NASA. I went swimming. I went to the beach. I surfed on waves. I went to the park. The shuttle was delayed so we had to go back home and watch it on TV.

My Wonderful World ... Traveling

Going to Disney World
By Sadie G.

My family took a trip to Disney World. We took Mom and Dad and Reiss. We went on lots of rides. It was lots of fun. We went on one of the rides over and over again. We had a fantastic time. We took a taxi and an airplane to get there. We went in 2008. Once in the hotel, we went to the pool. There was a hot tub and we went in it. It was fun, very fun!! Once we went to the lake. We rode bikes around the lake. One night, we ordered dinner in our hotel room. We had to wait a long time. The dinner was good.

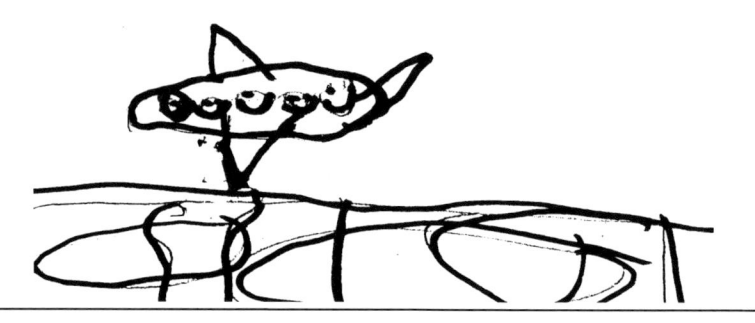

Going to Richmond
By Alexis B.

I went to Richmond. It was exciting! I couldn't wait! It was so much fun! It was a looooong car trip. I brought my babies and some toys with me. One was Teddy. One was Luxum and one was a duck. My mom and my daddy went with me in the car. It was fun in the car. I watched a movie.

By Ms. Hemstreet's Hippos

The Trip to Texas
By Lucy D..

I went to Texas. No one was left behind. I went with my whole family. We went last summer. I took a train to the airport. We went to see my grandma and grandpa. We stayed in a lake house and there was a beach. My grandma and grandpa have lots of toys. I went to the beach every day. Once I was trying to do a ballet move, but a wave knocked me down. It was fun. I even got to see cowboys. I got to ride a horse. It was awesome.

About the Beach
By Joaquin T.

I went to the beach with my dog. We went to the beach when I was three years old. We took a bus. We went just for fun. We went swimming next to the whales. They were little. It was not fun.

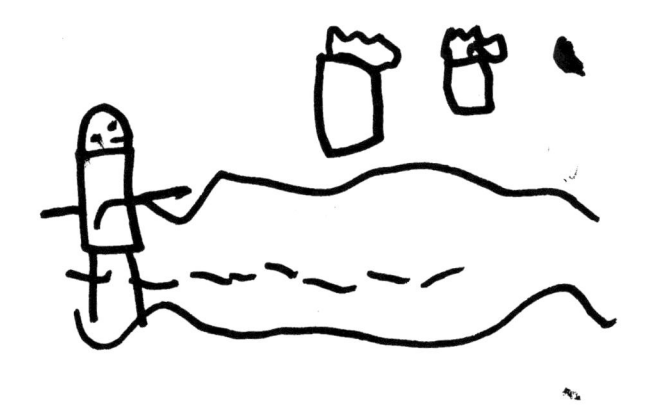

My Wonderful World ... Traveling

The Christmas Trip
By James K.

At Christmas time, Jenna and Grandma and me went to Disney World. We went on a plane. We went on rides. I went on Pirates of the Caribbean. I had fun on Lightning Railroad. It was fun, really fun. We went on a plane to get home. I slept on the plane. There was a comfy little head thing.

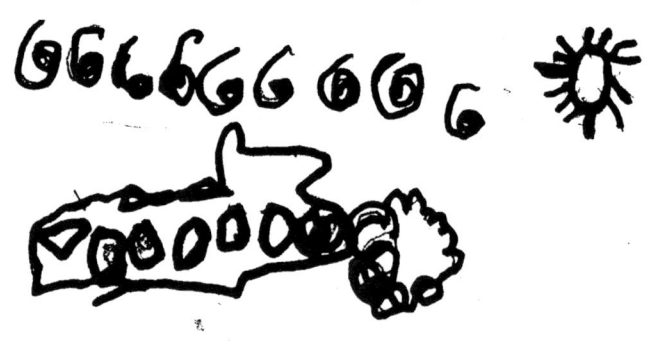

The Trip to Musgrove
By Ian V.

My family went to Musgrove on a plane. I went with my mom and dad and Luke and Aidan. We slept on the plane. It was fun. I went swimming. We bought a boogie board. We had fun. It was a long way home. The end.

By Ms. Hemstreet's Hippos

K

The Trip to the Beach
By Tyson P.

I went to the beach last summer with Mom, Dad, Tyler and Tyson. I took a car. When I got there, I played in the sand. I went to get ice cream. I got vanilla. There was a long line. One day, I built a sandcastle. I connected all the sandcastles and I made a square. My trip was a good trip.

Going to the Farm
By Bair P.

Mom, Dad, me, Keira and Willow went to the farm in a car. We took turns riding on a horse. It was fun. I love riding. Tony and Sally are the horse's names. I had clam chowder. Do you like clam chowder? I like clam chowder. Baba and Jaaj live at the farm. They are my grandparents.

My Wonderful World ... Traveling

Summer School
By Abi B.

In summer, I am going to take my car to my summer school. Awesome! I can't wait! It will be so fun. I will be in a different class. I hope I learn about candy. Yeah! I am going to meet some new friends. It will be fun. My teacher is going to like me because I share. My friend Avery is coming, too.

My Trip to the Beach
By Aidan M.

I am going to the beach. I am going in a big van. When I get there, I am going to beat up the crabs.

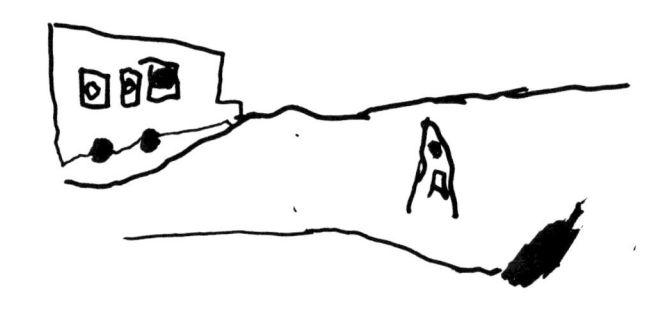

By Mrs. Howard's Warthogs

K

My Sister's Birthday
By Ava B.

I am going to Georgia by airplane. I am going with my mom and my sister for my sister's birthday. It is going to be springtime. I will bring my cat.

My Family is Going to San Francisco
By Billie L.

My friend is moving to San Francisco and I'm going on an airplane to see her. It is going to take five hours. When I get there, I will hug my friend in the snow. When it is almost time to go to bed, we will watch a show. Then we will go to bed and I will sleep in a sleeping bag with my bunny and my Baby Alive.

My Wonderful World ... Traveling

A Long Ride
By Colleen D.

I am going to New York by car. I am going over the weekend to see my friend Samantha. I am going to play with her.

I Am Going to North Carolina
By Devin G.

I am going to North Carolina in my mom's Mini Cooper. I am going in May because my dad wants to see his mom and I want to see my cousins. It will be so fun.

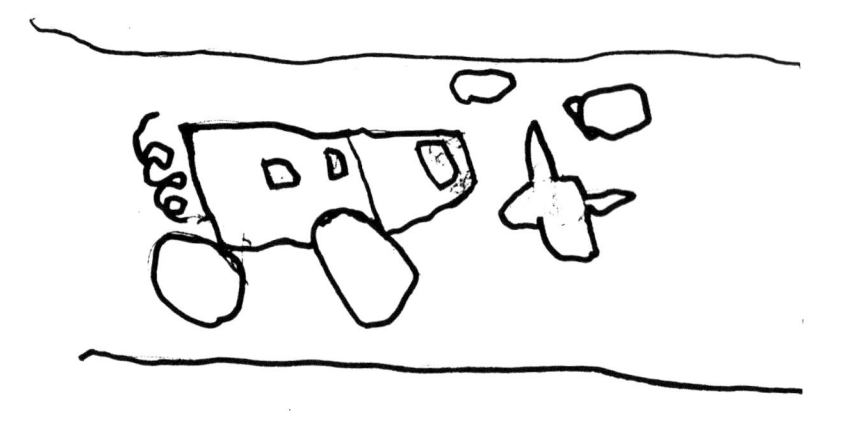

By Mrs. Howard's Warthogs

K

My Trip to the Beach
By Ella E.

I went by car to the beach. My grandparents come every time. I went to Atlanta Beach. It was fun. Mom and Dad and my brother came. I brought snacks and toys and blankets on my trip.

A Fun Trip
By Costas T.

Uncle Devin, white blanket, Great Wolf Lodge. I went in my car. It was one thousand minutes to get there. This was a perfect trip.

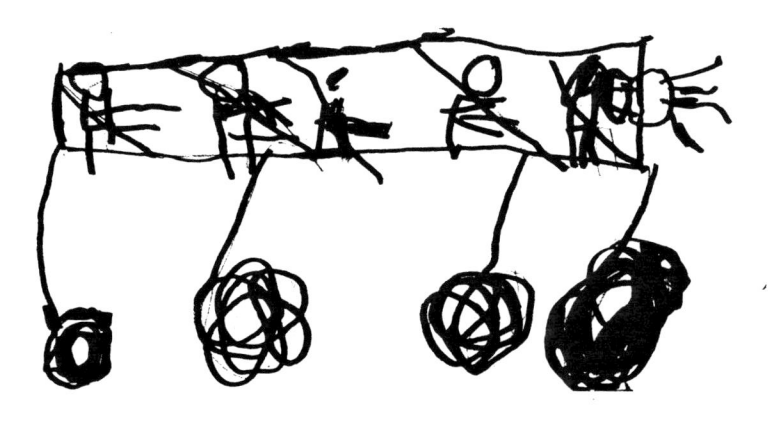

My Wonderful World ... Traveling

My Trip to North Carolina
By Ella G.

I went to North Carolina. It took a long time to get there, but it was fun. We went in my van. Then, when I got there, we went to the beach. It was fun.

The Big Truck
By Gwynni J.

Last year, I went to Australia. The suitcases had to be jumped on to make them close. After we jumped on the suitcases, we got on the plane and flew and flew and flew. But this year it was too expensive. In August I will go in a big truck to the beach. I will catch a crab. I will be in the water fighting the crabs.

By Mrs. Howard's Warthogs

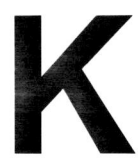

K

A Long Drive
By Joey P.

I went to North Carolina in a car. It was in winter. It took a long time to get there. I went to see my mom. I was so happy! Finally, I made it to North Carolina. I got up. I had a fun cabin. I dug in the sand and then I picked up my mom. The next morning, I watched the sun rise and got ready to go sailing.

I Am Going to Discover Another Galaxy
By John P.

I am going to another galaxy on another Earth. I am going with my babysitter in my super jet with yellow fire and green fire and orange fire. I will go and find some air and I will go and find more people. I will find food.

My Wonderful World ... Traveling

My Trip to Florida
By Kara B.

I went in my car to the airport. I went in the airplane to Florida. I was two. I brought clothes. My brother and my dad and my mom came along. My uncle was fun. I love my uncle. I went because I wanted to. Florida has rides. I went on a couple rides. I stayed for two days. On the next day, I flew home. I love my family!

The Big Trip
By Mito P.

I went to California. I got on an airplane. Mom, Max, Federico went with me. I went in 2008.

By Mrs. Howard's Warthogs

I Went By Airplane
By Natasha M.

In May, I am going to Florida and I am going by an airplane. It is going to take one hour. When I get there, I am going swimming. I will have a snack. I will take a nap. Then I will watch TV. Then I will go to bed. Then I will go home.

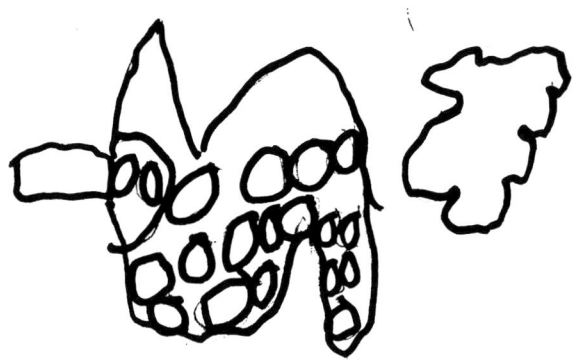

Going with Minty
By Nina S.

I am going to My Little Pony World. I will get there on a bike. It takes three minutes and the Pony I will ride is Minty.

My Wonderful World ... Traveling

My Trip to Australia
By Patrick C.

I went to Australia. I got there by a boat. It took me three days. It was a long trip. I went in January. We learned about saving crocodiles from fires. We also learned about putting out fires without water.

I Love the Snow
By Raquel R.

I went to the ski house. I got there by car. I went with my family. The name of the place is Wintergreen Resort in Virginia. When I got there, I played.

By Mrs. Howard's Warthogs

K

A Trip to Alaska
By Silas P.

I went to Alaska. I flew from Virginia to California. Then I took a boat to Alaska. I had a good time. I slipped down an icy hill.

My Medium Ride
By Simon K.

I went in a minivan to Maryland. Me, Peyton, Mom, Dad, and Benson went together. It was in 2009. It was almost Valentine's Day. We visited my grandma and grandpa. It was fun.

My Wonderful World ... Traveling

Flying to Texas
By Gibson L.

I went to Houston, Texas with my family. Dad, Mom, Griffin, Garrett and I are in my family. We went to visit my godmother. It was so hot in the winter that we could wear shorts and short sleeves. We came home on two airplanes and in a car. It was a great vacation.

The Trip to Chicago
By Carolyn S.

We went to a beautiful place, a city named Chicago. My whole family had fun on my trip when we unpacked our suitcases out of the car. We stayed in a hotel and ate in the restaurant there. We went the day after my birthday, February 5th, last year. Mommy wanted to go on the trip for a surprise.

By Mrs. Toner's Pooh Bears

My Trip to Jamaica
By Kate S.

I went to Jamaica when I was five in the summer with my Dad, Mom, Will and Doug. We went by car to the airport. Then we took two or three airplanes to get there. We went on blue, yellow and red waterslides. One was next to a coconut tree. We had delicious food. Even the dessert was great. Our room was beautiful. We saw some chickens walking around. There was a school. I got to choose if I wanted to go there or not. I went and it was great! I made rock castles on the beach. When I was in the water, I had to close my eyes because we didn't bring goggles. I washed up on the shore so I didn't have to walk on the pointy rocks. Jamaica was fun! Jamaica was great!

My Wonderful World ... Traveling

My Trip to Disney World
By Owen B.

Mom, Dad, Sophie, Eliza and I went to Disney World last summer. It was really hot. First, I went in my golden Acura to the airport. We got on a red, white and blue airplane. We got there and we went on roller coasters at Disney World. I always wanted to go there. We played until night. It was fun!

Our Trip to Virginia Beach
By Kathryn D.

Grandma, Mom, Dad, Parker, Jasper and I went to Virginia Beach when I was four. We always go in our car. Sometimes we stop and get Krispy Kreme doughnuts. I like to play in the water at the beach. I always make a new friend.

By Mrs. Toner's Pooh Bears

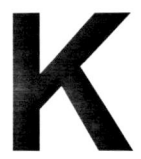

K

Going to Florida
By Eleanor G.

I went to Florida with Mommy and Dad and my little brother. We went in a car and in an airplane. I played with my cousins. It was fun. When I got home, I played with toys.

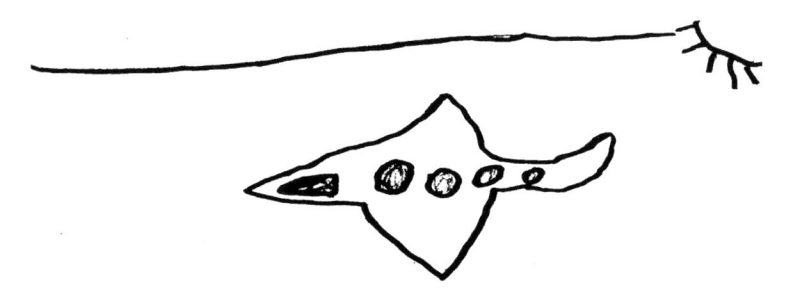

Learning to Ski
By Katie S.

I went to Utah in February. Andre, Marc, Mommy and Daddy went with me. My family went by car and plane. I learned to ski. Skiing was fun, except for the last day. It was tiring. After skiing, I ate a yummy lunch.

My Wonderful World ... Traveling

My Trip to the Virgin Islands
By Oliver S.

It was a special birthday for Mom. She was taking me, Grandma and Grandpa on a trip to the Virgin Islands. We had to get up very early. We took a taxi to the airport. The plane took us to Miami. Then we got on another plane that took us to where we got on a ferry. We ferried over to the island that we camped on. It had been a long trip, but we weren't there yet. We had to get in another taxi which was actually a bus. At last our holiday started. We went to the beach. I learned to snorkel. I saw lots of fish. I saw three barracudas. While we were there, the front office told us that a CAT 2 hurricane was coming. We had to get off our island and take the ferry to another island so we could be in a hotel and be safe. When we got to the hotel, I saw it had a good pool. I played and swam in the pool. What an exciting trip!

By Mrs. Toner's Pooh Bears

K

Going to France
By Hugo S.

I am going to France in a big airplane and a small airplane. It makes two airplanes. It will be a good and nice vacation. My Maman and Daddy are going to France with me. We will drive in a red car when we are there. Then we'll take it back to the car store. We will visit my grandma in France. Then we will come back to the United States of America.

Going to Miami
By Tony D.

I am going to Miami in June with my dad and mom, Sydney, Joe and Harry. We are going to take the car to the airport. Next, we are going to fly on the airplane. When we get there, we are going to play in the sand and go fishing. I hope it is an amazing vacation!

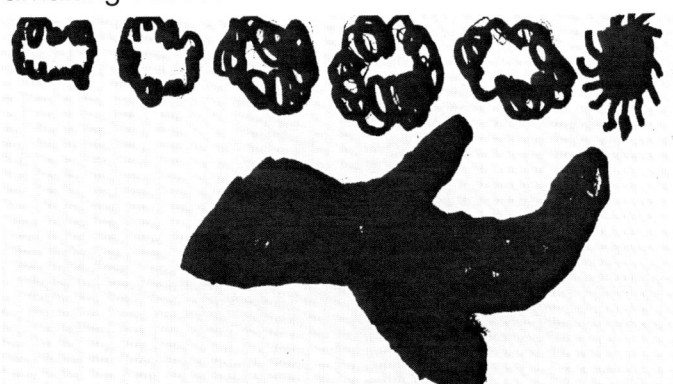

My Wonderful World ... Traveling

Christmas in the Woods
By Issac M.

Me and lots of my family on my dad's side went to North Carolina for Christmas. There were so many of us we needed two cars and one family came by plane. The house we stayed at was in the woods. It belongs to my grandma and grandpa. I played hide and seek with my aunt and cousins. We watched movies. On Christmas Eve, I used my dad's stocking from when he was a little boy to hang by the fireplace. Santa came! My dad had sent a note to tell him where we would be on Christmas Day. We played Frisbee with the new one I got for Christmas. I liked my vacation, Christmas in the woods.

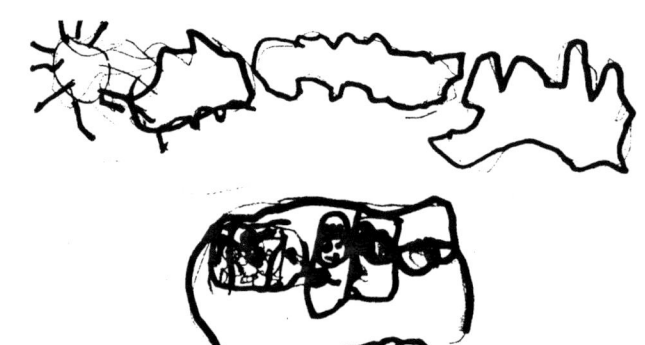

The Trip to Hawaii
By Laila F.

I went to Hawaii with Peggy, Gaga, Mom, Dad, Sam, Marisa and my two cousins. I went by car and by airplane. We had fun walking on the beach.

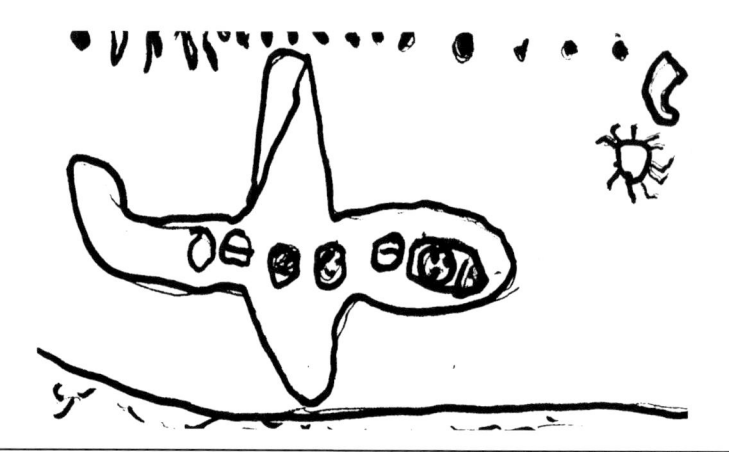

2009 © Nottingham Elementary School

By Mrs. Toner's Pooh Bears

K

At the Beach
By Gideon F.

I went to Ghana in 2004 when I was two. Me, Mommy and Daddy took two planes that were not 747s to get there. We went to London first and changed planes. We went to live there for Daddy's work. We went to the beach. It was hotter than Florida. I built a sandcastle. I played in the big waves and the warm water. I went swimming at my neighbor's house.

On the Beach
By Ethan B.

I went to Jamaica with my dad, my mom and Jake. We went on an airplane because Jamaica is an island in the Caribbean. We went last winter when it was cold in Arlington to have a family vacation. We rented a house that had a swimming pool. Jake and I had a swimming race with my dad. It was hot!

My Wonderful World ... Traveling

Going to Florida
By Logan M.

In April, I went to Florida with my mom and my brother, Peter. We were meeting up with relatives for a vacation. My cousins live there. We stayed at their house. They have a pool in their backyard. We went by car. We stopped for food on the way and didn't get there until nighttime. I had a good time there 'cause it was so fun.

Going to Nantucket!
By Julian D.

I am going to Nantucket! Dad, Mom, Adam, Leo and I are going in August this summer. We will go in a car, two planes and a van to get to our house. One of my favorite activities on Nantucket Island is playing at the beach. We go swimming, build sandcastles and eat ice cream!

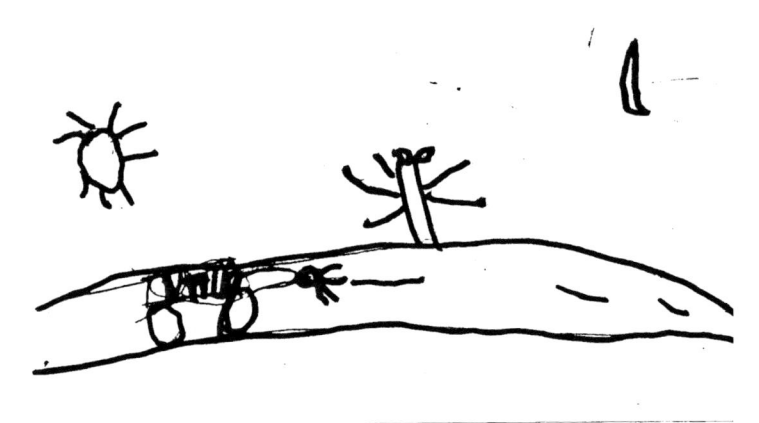

By Mrs. Toner's Pooh Bears

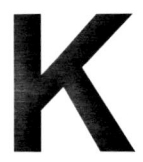

K

Going to the Beach
By Dari K.

I am going to the beach with Mama, Dada, Alex and Gretchen. It will be lots of fun once we get there. Fun! Fun! Fun! We will go in the summer. We will go in our white van. It will take forty hours to get there. When I get there, I will make sandcastles. I will splash my mom and dad in the ocean. I will have a good time!

Going Skiing
By Jennifer O.

In February, I went for a long weekend trip to Seven Springs with my mom and dad. Seven Springs is in Pennsylvania. We went by car. It took a long time to get there. We stayed at a nice hotel that had an indoor swimming pool. The water was deep, but I could swim in it. We went there to ski. I have been skiing before and liked it. I had a private lesson at the ski school. I fell down a couple of times, but I had fun. They made snow at the ski field. I had hot chocolate.

My Wonderful World ... Traveling

I Am Going to Norway
By Emma S.

Hi! My name is Emma! I flew on a plane with my mom, my dad, my sister and my brother to Norway. I got to watch Sleeping Beauty on the TV, but the headphones didn't fit me so I couldn't hear the sounds. We went to live in Norway because of my dad's job. I had fun going with my dad to his office. My family got our dog, Bjorn, in Norway. His name means "bear" in Norwegian.

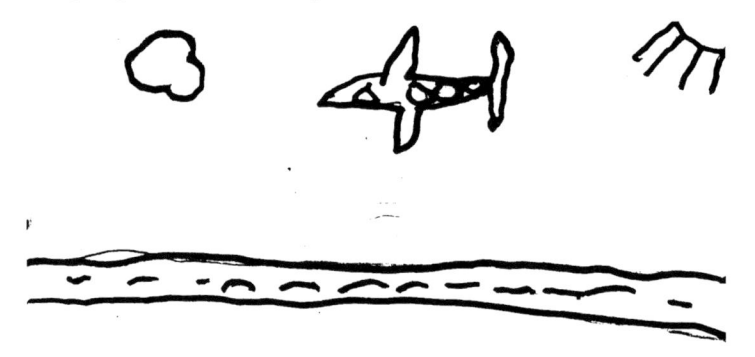

The Best Trip Ever!
By Elizabeth P.

I am going to Chautauqua, N.Y. in August with Mom, Dad, Zach and John. I am going in a car. I know I will have fun. We will play in the water and build sandcastles. We will get ice cream and watch plays. We will run free in the plaza and climb on the water fountain. You're allowed to. We will have fun. When it's time to leave, we will load up and go. We will stop in the car to get something to eat. Then we will drive on. See you next year, Chautauqua!

By Mrs. Toner's Pooh Bears

Flower Girl
By Taylor L.

I went to New Orleans with my Mom. Cousin Chrissy was getting married and I was going to be a flower girl for the first time. Mommy drove us to the airport. It took two planes to get there. We left early in the morning so I took a nap on the first plane. But on the second plane, I watched a movie. On the day of the wedding, I had butterflies in my tummy. I was excited. My dress was black with sparkles. I had a wreath of pink roses in my hair and I carried a basket of flowers. At the party afterwards, I was the best dancer. Everyone was taking pictures and movies of me. It was a fun weekend.

My Wonderful World

The Sky
By Olivia J.

The sky is blue.
The sky is pink.
The sky is black.
The sky has stars.
The sky has a big sun.
The sun gives us brightness.
I love the sky!

Snakes
By Graham P.

Snakes are hard to spot
And are great climbers.
Sometimes poisonous,
And very scary.
They have extremely sharp teeth,
Often heavy,
Found in the wild jungle.

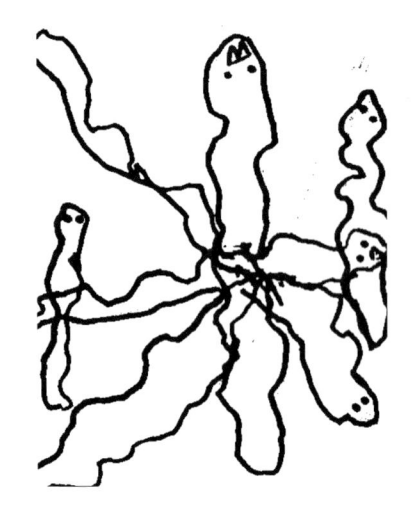

By Ms. Gassman's Lovebugs

1

Flags
By Chris H.

Flags can be red, white,
And blue.
The stars are white.
The wind makes the flag
Float.

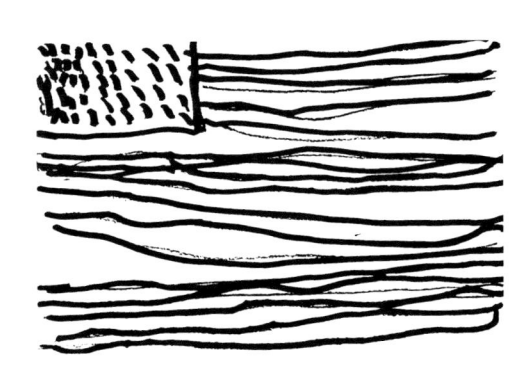

Mud
By Emma W.

Mud is
Dirty,
Not so
Clean,
Very
Squishy,
Muddy,
Slippery in my hands.

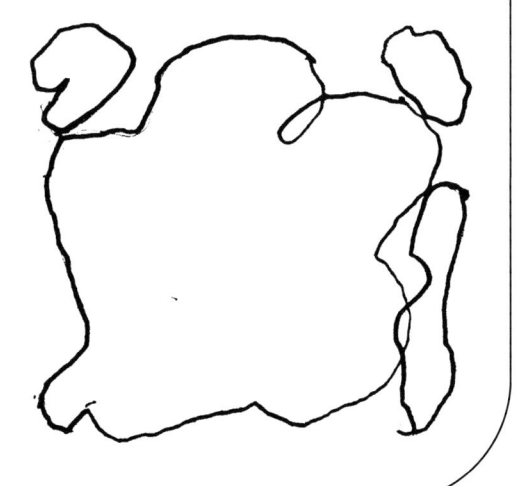

My Wonderful World

Jack the Bat
By Eamon S.

Jack has green eyes,
Soft wings,
Cuddly black fur.
He is a bat.

Football
By Noah L.

Football,
Sign up.
Football,
Pick what team.
Football,
Play your best.
Football,
Touch down!
Football,
Win the game.
Football,
In the Hall of Fame.
Football!

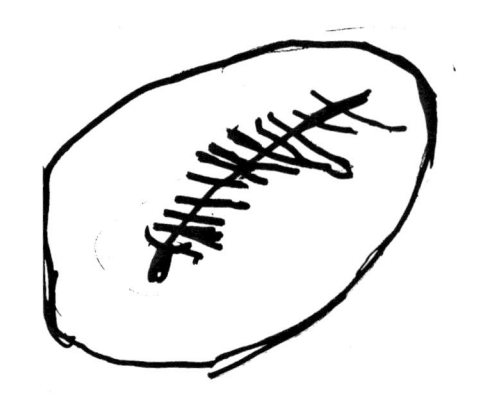

By Ms. Gassman's Lovebugs

Slime
By Max P.

Slime is gooey.
Slime is as green as grass.
Slime is as soft as a quilt.
Slime is a liquid just like water.
   SPLASH!
I like it.

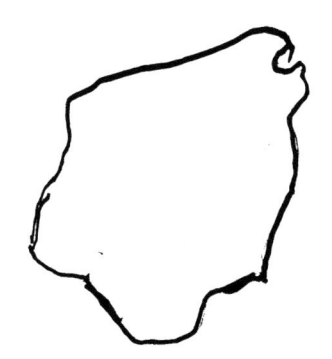

Roads
By Jacob C.

Roads can take you far.
Roads are long.
Roads are short.
Roads are huge.
Roads are teeny.
Roads are thin.
Roads are thick.
I like roads!

My Wonderful World

I Like ...
By Maddy T.

I like
New toys,
My name,
Family fun,
Drawing cities,
My pet fish,
My diary ...
And you,
Even Webkinz, too!

My Dogs
By Addie A.

You make me feel like I
Have food for free.
You hunt for ducks, birds,
And other things you see.
You're very energetic and loyal.
You're always barking when Dad comes home.
Justice and Liberty are my dogs ...
Dogs, dogs, dogs!

By Ms. Gassman's Lovebugs

Chocolate
By Cynthia D.

Scrumptious, delicious,
Crunchy, brown,
Melty, smooth,
No nuts -
I finished mine,
How about you?
I like chocolate!

Wind
By Mousa M.

Cold wind,
Strong wind,
Invisible wind,
Pushy wind,
Shhhhhh! - Shhhhh!

My Wonderful World

Smoothies
By Eli W.

I drank a smoothie.
It was delicious.
It tasted like mashed up
Cherries and blueberries.
You should try one, too.
"Yum, yum!" I said,
And I hope
You say it, too!

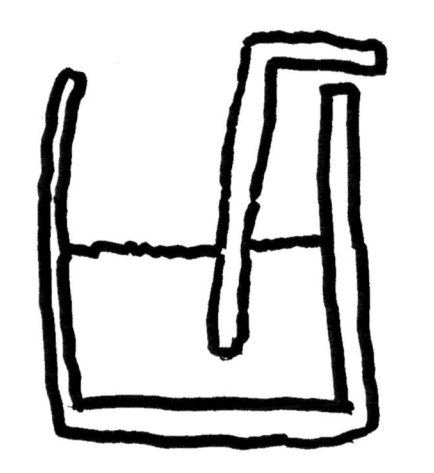

Stuffy, My Dog
By Lily D.

Doggy, doggy,
Falling apart.
Doggy,
I still love you no matter what.
The string is unwrapping,
I am holding him tight.
I hope I can sleep with him
Every night!

By Ms. Gassman's Lovebugs

Number 5
By Brook S.

5, 5,
I was 5.
He, he,
He was 5.
They, they,
They were 5.
We, we,
We were 5.
5, 5, 5, 5, 5, 5, 5, 5, 5, 5, 5!

Blue
By Sophie S.

Blue bow is clipped on your head.
Blue, blue, everywhere!
Warm water is blue.
My cold chair is blue.
Are you feeling blue?
No, I am not!
I am excited.
Blue!

My Wonderful World

Flowers
By Keely P.

Flowers,
Colorful,
Grows in the grass,
Green, too!
I like flowers.
How about you?

Ice Cream
By Natalie E.

Cold, melting stuff.
Chocolate, strawberry and vanilla,
Circular, drippy stuff.
Triangular, crunchy cone.
Puffy ice cream,
Yummy, ice cream!

By Ms. Gassman's Lovebugs

Bora Bora
By Will S.

I feel …
The sun,
  Free,
Happy,
  Sweet,
  Wetness,
And the clear, warm water.

I see …
The sandy beaches,
  Lots of water,
  Fun houses,
  Coconut trees,
  Colorful coral,
And leaping dolphins.

Piranhas
By Michael Z.

Three, three, I was three.
Bit, bit … I got bit.
Scared, scared … I got scared.
Dad, Dad … Dad was sad.
Me, me … me was three.
Three, three, when I was three!

My Wonderful World ... Animals

Baby Humpback Whales
By Allison S.

The baby humpback whale is 14 feet long. It is born alive and drinks its mother's milk. When baby whales get bigger, they like to eat tiny animals called krill. Humpback whales migrate. They live in warm tropical oceans in the winter. Then they travel to cold polar waters in the summer to find food. Humpback whales like to stay at the top of the water but can dive for 30 minutes without air! Humpback whales are an endangered species.

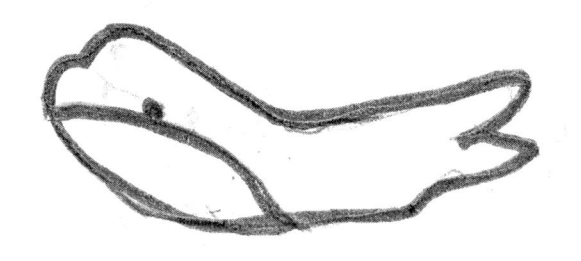

Cardinals
By Maggie L.

Cardinals are the state bird of Virginia. Cardinals are the color of Valentine cards. They live in trees and bushes and like to eat sunflower seeds, fruits and berries. Cardinals are herbivores. Cardinals have feathers and use their wings to fly. Baby cardinals are hatched from eggs.

By Mrs. Jensen's Jolly Rogers

Turtles
By Gavin M.

The turtle has four strong legs and a hard shell on its back. The shell has colors that help it blend into the background. Turtles are reptiles and they hatch from eggs. Turtles live on every continent except Antarctica. Turtles have a sharp beak they use to eat food. Turtles eat plants, crickets and worms.

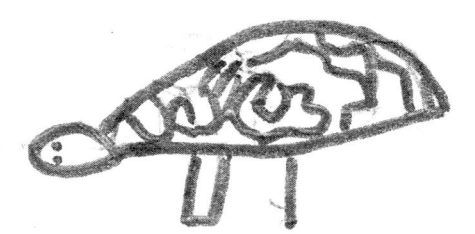

Zebras
By Casey B.

Each zebra has its own pattern of stripes. No two zebras have the same pattern. Zebras are mammals and live in the wilds of Africa. There are three kinds of zebras. There is the Grevy's zebra, the Plains zebra and the Mountain zebra. Zebras like to eat grasses, shrubs, herbs and bark. The foods that zebras eat are too hard for their teeth so their teeth fall out and new teeth grow in their place. Zebras are herbivores.

My Wonderful World ... Animals

Cheetahs
By Sam B.

The cheetah is a mammal. It is an endangered animal. The cheetah lives in Africa in the savannas. Cheetahs are carnivores. They like to eat antelope, rabbits and birds. Cheetahs run very fast to catch their food. A grown up cheetah can run as fast as 60 mph.

The Rhino
By Alec R.

The rhino is the second largest land mammal. It can weigh one to one and a half tons. Rhinos have two horns and are gray. A young rhino is called a calf. Rhinos mark their home with their scent. Rhinos are herbivores. They eat grasses, fruit and plants. They live on the grasslands of Africa.

By Mrs. Jensen's Jolly Rogers

Giraffes
By Brenna N.

A giraffe's tongue is purplish black and can be 18 inches long! It uses its long tongue to eat leaves from a tall tree. They are herbivores. Giraffes can run as fast as 35 mph. The giraffe is a mammal. The neck of a giraffe can be more than 5 feet long! Tick birds like to climb up and down the long neck of the giraffe. These birds like to eat the ticks found on the giraffe. The body covering of a giraffe is brown and white dotted fur. Giraffes are mammals.

The Koala
By Aly L.

The koala is a wild animal. It lives in Australia where there are plenty of eucalyptus trees. The koala has soft brown and gray fur. Koalas can be three feet tall and weigh up to 20 pounds. Koalas are mammals and the babies are called joeys. They live in their mother's pouch for about seven months.

My Wonderful World ... Animals

Horses
By Eva G.

Horses are mammals. Most horses are born at night. The horse moves its ears, eyes and nostrils to show its feelings. Horses are measured by using hands, and a hand is about four inches. A horse can gallop, trot and walk. Horses live in pastures or stables. They love to eat apples and oats.

Spitting Cobra
By Bennett C.

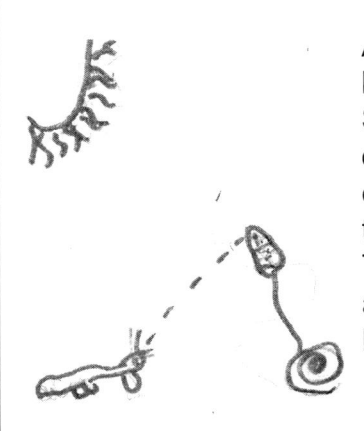

A spitting cobra will puff out its skin to look like a hood to scare predators. Spitting cobras live in the warm climates of Egypt and Africa. Spitting cobras don't spit out their venom. They spray their venom into the eyes of their prey. The venom causes blindness. Cobras are reptiles and will eat other snakes, birds and other small mammals.

By Mrs. Jensen's Jolly Rogers

1

Huskies
By Anne B.

Huskies are mammals and they are working dogs. They pull sleds for racing and to help people. They are very fast runners. Huskies are very strong and large. Huskies are trained and live with people.

Penguins
By Vittoria T.

Penguins live in Antarctica. They are not cold when they are in the sea or on the snow. Their feathers and fat help penguins to stay warm. Penguins are four feet tall when they are grown up, but they are only four inches tall when they are born. Penguins love to play in the sea and are very social.

My Wonderful World ... Animals

King Cobras
By Patrick C.

I think King Cobras are cool. They live in Asia. They can stand tall enough to look you straight in in the eye. The King Cobra eats snakes. It sleeps with its eyes open.

Lions
By Karl N.

Lions are mammals and they live in Asia and Africa. Lions are in the tall grasses of the savannah and they like to rest under a shady tree. Lions have sharp teeth. They use their sharp teeth to catch and bite their prey. Lions like to eat wildebeest, zebras, giraffes and antelopes. They are carnivores. The male lion also has a large mane of fur around his head.

By Mrs. Jensen's Jolly Rogers

Penguins
By Elliot E.

Penguins are birds that cannot fly. They have feathers and lay eggs. An Emperor penguin keeps its egg on the top of its toes near his belly so the egg won't get cold. Penguins have to walk very slowly so the egg won't fall off and touch the cold ground. Penguins do not hibernate. They live in a big colony in Antarctica. Penguins like to eat fish, but they have to be very careful because leopard seals and killer whales live in the ocean and they love to eat PENGUINS!

Manatees
By Jena K.

Manatees are mammals. They have wrinkled skin and are a gray brown color. They live in warm water and there are more manatees in Florida than anywhere else. Manatees grow to be 10-11 feet and can weigh over 1,500 pounds. Manatees like to eat seaweed and other plants.

My Wonderful World ... Animals

Orca Whales
By Dean J.

The Orca whale has smooth wet skin. It is black and white. Orca whales are mammals and they are much bigger than humans. The Orca lives in the ocean and lives in families called pods. Orca whales like to eat squid, fish and penguins. Orcas like to migrate to warmer water when the water gets too cold.

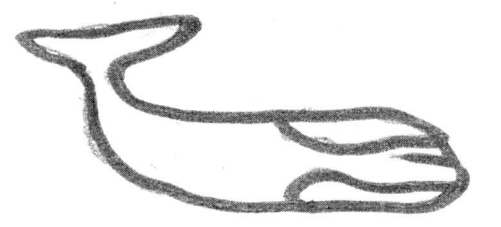

King Cobra
By Donovan T.

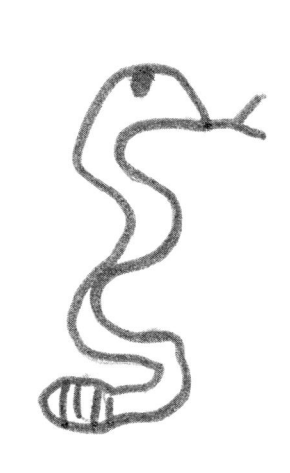

The cobra has shiny skin and color patterns on its body. Cobras are five or six feet long. They are hatched from eggs and are cold-blooded. They are reptiles. Cobras are carnivores. They like to eat mice, lizards, birds, frogs and other snakes! Cobras do not chew their food. They swallow their food whole. Cobras like to live in the jungle.

By Mrs. Jensen's Jolly Rogers

Koalas
By Anna G.

Koalas sleep in the day time because they are nocturnal. Most people think koalas are just lazy, but they are just nocturnal. At night they eat food. When koalas are born, the joeys are small, pink, and hairless. They feel their way to their mother's pouch. Koalas eat eucalyptus leaves. Eucalyptus leaves are poison to most animals, but not koalas.

My Wonderful World

The Diplodocus
By Jeremy L.

Diplodocus, diplodocus,
In the hay
And it is gray.
Happy! Happy dinosaur
Until the time that
The asteroid
Hit the earth.
He was 88 feet long.

Pink Blanket
By Emma M.

I'm a blanket.
I am pink and fuzzy.
I'm soft and little.
I sleep with my owner.
I love
My owner!
It makes me happy
To sleep with my owner.

By Ms. Kepchar's Kangaroos

Jack
By Alex M.

My brother,
He sleeps downstairs.
He likes to bring toys to school.
He likes his mommy.
He likes to play
Video games.
My brother
Likes to watch TV.

Loose Tooth
By Sophie K.

I have a loose tooth,
But it won't come out.
Come out,
Come out,
Come out,
Tooth.
If you don't,
I'll yank you out.
I'll yank and yank
Until you come out!
Tooth Fairy,
Tooth Fairy,
Please, please come and
Give me a quarter,
One by one.

My Wonderful World

Cats
By Maggie D.

So puffy on their
Tails
Can be
Black
Mine is
Fat
Sleeps by my
Toes.
Did you
Know?
Such
Cute
Noses
Mine sits by the
Fireplace.
Did you know?

Snowflakes
By Marion L.

Falling snow goes all around.
It's like a rainbow bending.
It looks like a princess.
It looks pretty.
It looks as pretty as a princess.
I love the snow.

By Ms. Kepchar's Kangaroos

Biscuit
By Emma G.

Bingo's biscuit is large.
She ate it all up.
Yum, yum, biscuit!
Bingo eats it up.
She licks it up!
Munch, munch!
Crunch, crunch!
Bingo eats it up!
She munches it up!
Yum, yum.
What a good dog!
I love her.

Aunt Melanie
By Allison S.

Aunt Melanie is so nice.
She gives me Webkinz,
It's so nice.
She even gives me Webkinz
That my mom and dad
Don't know about.
When my Mom and Dad
Find out,
They call Aunt Melanie and say …
"She has enough Webkinz!
Give her some later
When she loses some."
"No," she says,
"No!"

My Wonderful World

My Favorite Food
By Ricardo C.

It sounds like nothing.
It comes separated, but I mix it.
It tastes yummy.
Chicken is light brown and yellow.
Rice is white.
It is moo shu,
Moo shu chicken and rice.

The Marble
By Anna K.

It looks like there's a snake inside,
A poisonous snake that gives you cancer.
The poisonous snake that is slimy and gooey,
That poisonous snake that can eat you up!
The poisonous snake that is brave and strong,
That poisonous snake,
Fearless,
That never cries.
That poisonous snake,
Evil and nasty!

By Ms. Kepchar's Kangaroos

1

My Brother
By Isabel F.

Not much hair,
But cute brown eyes,
Red mouth,
White top,
Blue, soft, silky pants
With orange crabs.
Rock and roll shoes.
I love my brother.

Me
By Ethan L.

I am a champion
And unique,
But I don't like pie!
I like PG-13 movies
And Speed Racer,
Indiana Jones,
And Star Wars!
I like ships.
I like chocolate.
It
Tastes
Good.
I am
Ethan.

My Wonderful World

My Parrot
By Lara C.

My parrot copies me,
Loves people,
Is my pet,
Plays with treats,
Loves pictures,
Nibbles my finger.
I am proud
Of my parrot.

My Hamster
By Dorin K.

My hamster is so quick.
She climbs on a climbing stick.
Her climbing cage
Is like a stage.
Is it me?
The really good hamster?
That does run and has so much fun?
Yes, it is!

By Ms. Kepchar's Kangaroos

Jingle Jangle
By Jack N.

Jingle, jangle,
Christmas lights,
All around the
Neighborhood site.
Christmas trees
For you and me.
Winter is great,
When spring is late.

The Paper Clip
By Luke R.

Big and small and medium,
Paper clip.
The arches look like
Two mountains.
It is shaped
Like an oval.
One clips to
Another one.
So very, very neat.
Different colors.
Oh, so beautiful.
I love it so much.
It is like a beaut.

My Wonderful World

Lobster
By Dylan H.

You are yummy.
You live in the ocean.
You are the best
In Maine!!!

Clip
By Maya C.

It is big and
Smooth and
It is red and
It looks
Curvy.
It's so large that
You can play
With it.
You can put
So
Much
Paper in it.

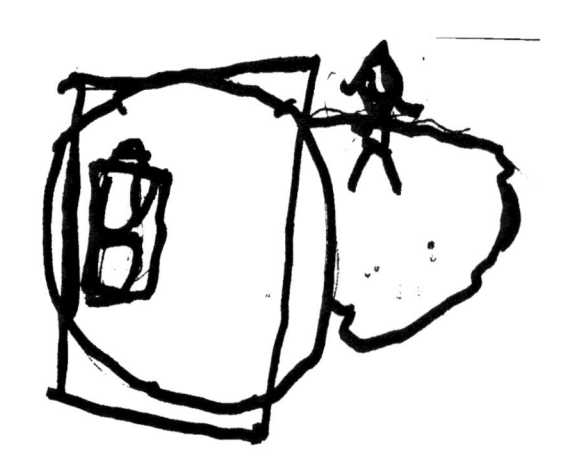

By Ms. Kepchar's Kangaroos

Christmas Time
By Jared B.

Jingle, jangle, Christmas lights
Light up the night.
Happy people so loud,
Jolly kids so proud.
Jingle, jangle, Christmas tree,
Santa Claus,
Here
He'll
Be.

Taking a Bath
By Sean S.

Splashing,
Splashing,
Taking a bath.
All bubbly,
Soapy,
Hot,
Cozy,
Taking a bath is fun.

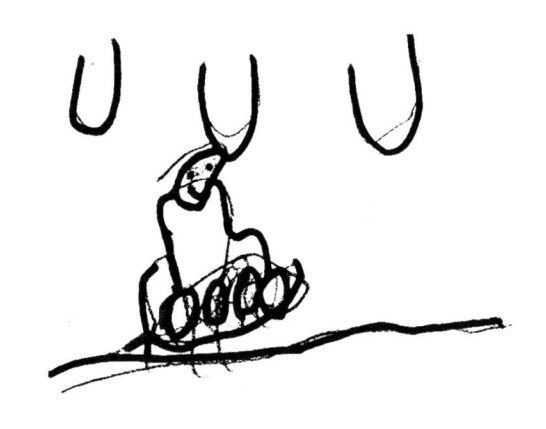

My Wonderful World

Butterflies
By Jacob H.

I have wings that fly,
Swish,
In the wind,
Real high in the wind.
But first I start out as a little caterpillar.
But before I am a caterpillar,
I am an egg that hatches.
CRACKKKK!

Pumpkins
By Emma S.

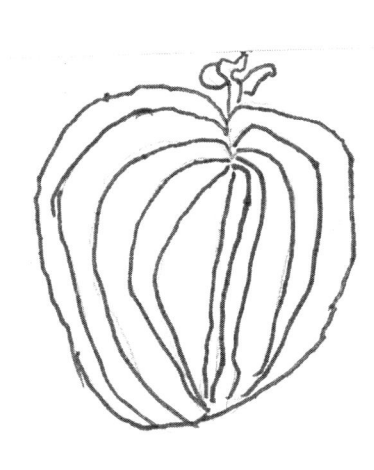

P-u-m-p-k-i-n-s,
Pumpkin time is here again.
Big ones, round ones,
Small ones, too.
Pick one out that's right for you.
P-u-m-p-k-i-n-s,
Pumpkin time is here again!

By Mrs. Lee's Elephants

1

My Desk
By Joseph P.

My desk is dirty.
My desk is sweet.
My desk is friendly
Where snacks are
Perfect to eat.

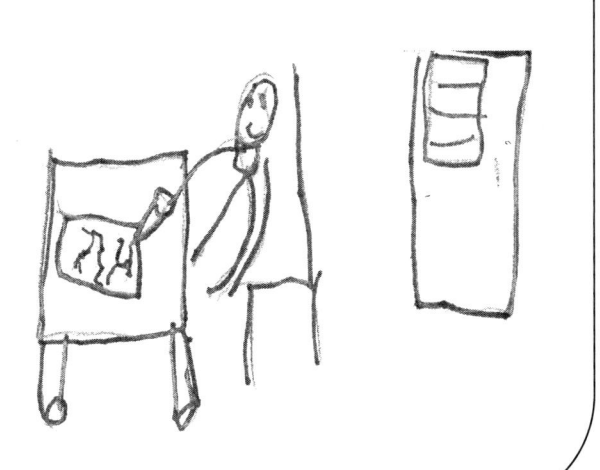

How to Make a Poem
By Wes L.

2 cups fun,
1 cup laugh,
4 cups adventure,
1 cup sad,
5 cups happy,
Get a spoon,
Mix it up,
With some interesting words,
And a dash of onomatopoeia,
And a pinch of rhythm,
And there's a poem!

My Wonderful World

The Wind
By Charlotte P.

The wind
Is
Smooth.
It looks as
If
It is gliding
Through the air
In the painting.

Snow
By Christy L.

Falling snow,
Coming here and there.
So white I can only stare.
Swirling around and around
In the sky.

2009 © Nottingham Elementary School

By Mrs. Lee's Elephants

Megan
By Abby T.

Megan is mean.
I love her anyway.
She is the best
I can tell you that, too.
I love her so much.
She is the best.
She makes me so happy,
That I can even cry!

Scariest Night
By Charlotte B.

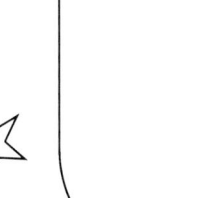

Vampires screaming
In fright.
Ghosts are flying,
Scariest night!

My Wonderful World

Fires
By Charlie B.

Fires are dangerous.
Fires are important
To get out of the house.
Stop, drop and roll.
Hurry up!
The fire is coming towards you!

Flowers
By Alice B.

Flowers bloom in spring
So beautiful.
But…
In the winter
They fade away.
I hope they
Come another spring.

2009 © Nottingham Elementary School

By Mrs. Lee's Elephants

Cats
By Grace C.

Cats sleep
Anywhere
Cats sleep
Up
  On
    The
      Piano
        Down
          Under
            The
      Bed, cozy and
          Warm.
Oh, I love cats!

I Love My House
By Emma J.

I love my house. I love my house.
Yes, I do.
And if I leave…
I will be blue.
So please, Mom, Dad
Don't make us leave.
I love my house.
Yes, I do.

My Wonderful World

The Reindeer
By Primo S.

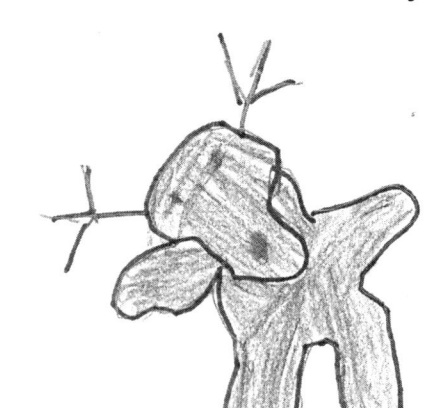

The reindeer
On a sled,
Up in the air,
With my dear Santa Claus.
Landing safely,
Thanks, Santa Claus,
My dear Santa Claus.

Raining
By Kara K.

Raining! Raining!
Drip! Drop!
The rain turns
Me blue.
Sun come out!
R-a-i-n, go away!
Do you hear me?

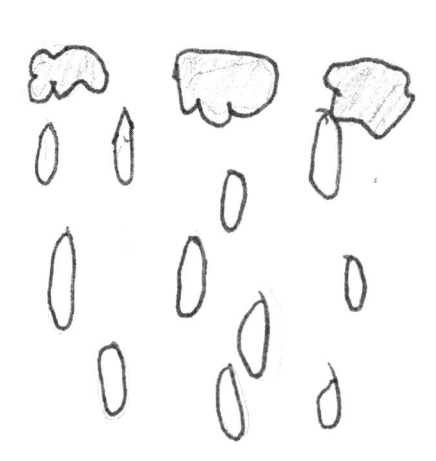

By Mrs. Lee's Elephants

Clay
By Kevin G.

Clay is like brown dough,
It feels like clean mud,
It smells like an old banana,
It sounds like squish,
It tastes like … oh, never mind!

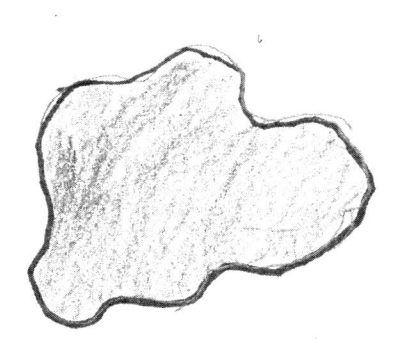

Music
By Jacob W.

Music is nice
And it has sound
So nice, like a violin.
Thank you for music.

My Wonderful World

My Dog Guinness
By Rosemary C.

My dog Guinness is very old.
My dog Guinness is not very bold.
My dog Guinness shakes and shakes
When thunderstorms are near.
My dog Guinness loves to go out
Again and again.
She lies on the grass
Staring into space
Watching the clouds.
I love my dog Guinness.

Dragons
By Will P.

We are frightening.
We are horrible and
We will eat you up
In a flash.
So, you beware.

By Mrs. Lee's Elephants

The Sun
By Jonathan D.

People wake as I slowly
Rise over the horizon,
Then
  I
    Slowly
      Fade
        Away.

Sven
By William T.

Look at Sven
Looking back
At me.
Look at Sven
We are playing the
"I'm Not Paying Attention
To You" game.

Let's Discover ... Animals

My Dog
By Hannah B.

The animal I chose to observe was my dog, Princess. Princess is a Yorkshire terrier. Princess lives inside my house. Sometimes she likes to go outside.

Usually my dog Princess likes to lie down on the couch or run around. Princess eats bones and dog food. I think she likes the bones the best.

I like Princess because she's small, quick, cute and smart. She's always so happy and she loves it when I pet her. Princess is the best pet ever!

Brownie the Bunny
By Elizabeth P.

The animal I chose to observe was a bunny. The bunny's name is Brownie. Brownie lives in a hole in my backyard. Brownie has four babies!

Brownie hops around the yard. It's soooo cute. My sister and I feed Brownie and her babies carrots.

I like Brownie because she is very cute. I also like Brownie because she is very pretty. Bunnies interest me because they're so nice, friendly and soooo cute. I love Brownie!

By Mr. Flood's Falcons

Fox Resource
By Geoffrey O.

The animal I chose to observe was a fox. Foxes live in bushes, in parks, in trees and in backyards.

A fox eats mice, rats, bugs, frogs and toads. Foxes hunt their food.

I like foxes because they have my favorite color on them and they hunt their food.

Leroy
By Macy M.

The animal I chose to observe was my dog, Leroy. He lives in my house sometimes. He sleeps in my bed. But sometimes he goes in my mom and dad's room or my sister's room. But mostly, he sleeps with me.

Leroy eats dog food and bones. One time, he ate a bird. My mom said we couldn't pet him because he ate a bird. My dog loves to run, but mostly he walks. He runs to get his food. He loves to chase my cat Little Kim, but Little Kim hisses at him and Leroy runs away.

I like Leroy because Leroy loves to sleep on the bed and sometimes he sleeps on my feet. He loves to lick me. The reason why he is interesting is because he is kind to Bryce, our other dog, and he does the same things as Bryce.

Let's Discover ... Animals

My Fish Lilly
By Camille P.

The animal I chose to observe was a Beta fish. Her name is Lilly. Lilly lives in a six quart bowl in water. At the bottom of the bowl, there are marbles.

Lilly swims slowly. Lilly eats these little pellets.

I like Lilly because she swims through hoops. She's scared of a wooden fish.

Rocko the Frog
By CJ O.

Rocko lives in a cage. The cage is filthy. Rocko likes to hide.

Rocko gets confused. He eats rocks and then he spits them out.

I like frogs like Rocko because they have big bubbly eyes!!

Dogs
By Megan C.

The animal I chose to observe was my dog named Shadow. He lives in a house and a crate.

My dog Shadow will play fetch and lay down. He eats dog food. We put it in a food bowl.

I like my dog because he is black, small, handsome, shiny and he has short hair. But most of all, he is a puppy!

By Mr. Flood's Falcons 2

Ducks
By David F.

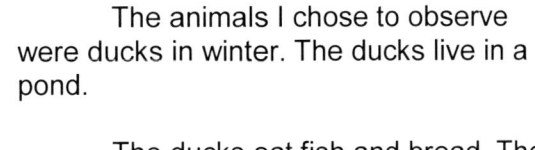

The animals I chose to observe were ducks in winter. The ducks live in a pond.

The ducks eat fish and bread. They get their food by diving underwater and from people.

I like ducks because they are funny and playful.

My Dog Weber
By Lindsey B.

The animal I chose to observe was my dog, Weber. Weber is a beagle. Sometimes Weber goes in his crate. But most of the time, Weber is somewhere in my house. I take him on walks and he is very adorable and loving.

Weber is very playful. He sometimes plays with his friend Augie. Weber is very loud and eats dog food.

I like Weber very much because he plays with me. It makes me happy.

Let's Discover ... Animals

My Dog Juno
By Joe D.

The animal I chose to remember was my dog, Juno. Juno lived in a cage when he was alive.

Juno ate cookies. He moved fast and he jumped.

I liked my dog Juno because he hunted food for us.

Mr. Crab
By Ben H.

The animal I chose to observe was my hermit crab, Mr. Crab. Mr. Crab lives in a cage.

Mr. Crab crawls to move and he eats Neapolitan cookies!

I like my hermit crab because he does not pinch. He is interesting because he can run!!

By Mr. Flood's Falcons

Spooky Bat
By Nick M.

The animal I chose to observe was a bat. My animal lives under the shingles of my house, but sometimes it goes in the trees.

The bat flies and it eats insects.

I like the bat because it's black. It skims across my pool and it looks really cool! The bat looks spooky, too. The bat has large ears.

Oscar
By Virginia H.

The animal I chose to observe was my cat, Oscar. He lives in our house. He sometimes goes outside.

Oscar likes to leap on the couch and sit next to me. He loves tuna and smells like it, too.

I like my cat Oscar because he is very nice to me. He is interesting because he is my pet and that is cool to me.

Let's Discover ... Animals

Coco
By Brendan J.

The animal I chose to observe was my dog, Coco. She lives in the house most of the time, but sometimes goes outside.

Coco eats food that my mom feeds her.

I like Coco because she is cute.

Birds
By Eli Z.

My animal lives in my backyard and in the neighborhood. In the backyard, the birds go in a tree. In the neighborhood, the birds fly all over the place.

Birds eat birdseed, bugs and insects. Birds fly and peck. They get food from a bird feeder.

I like birds because they fly and because they are small.

By Mr. Flood's Falcons

April
By Noah W.

April is the animal I chose to observe. She is a dog. My dog lives in the yard and in the house.

I feed April dog food every day. April lays around a lot.

I like April because she is sweet, shaggy and beautiful.

Dakota
By Madeleine H.

The animal I chose to observe was my dog, Dakota. He mostly lives inside, but sometimes outside. He sleeps on his special dog bed.

Dakota barks, scratches and licks. He eats kibble and green beans.

I like Dakota because he's soft, cuddly and smart. He's interesting because he chases his tail.

Let's Discover ... Animals

Sarg
By Ben K.

The animal I chose to observe was Gramma and Grampa's dog. His name is Sarg and he is a puppy. Sarg is very playful. Sarg lives most of the time in the house. Sarg is very jumpy and he likes to chase balls. Sarg always follows me around when he is off his leash.

Sarg eats dog food. When we go down to meet him, we change his water.

I like Sarg because he licks me all over when we get close. He likes to play with us and he jumps on me. His favorite thing to do with me is play hockey.

My Dog Bingo
By Jack G.

My dog, Bingo, lives in my house most of the time. I will put Bingo on the chain and she is strong, slow and nice.

Bingo walks on all fours and Bingo eats dog food.

I like my pet because she's cute. I wonder what she does at night.

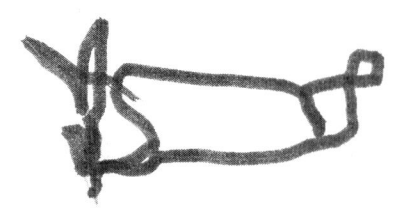

By Mr. Flood's Falcons 2

The Cardinal
By Stathi S.

The animal I chose to observe was a cardinal. It lives in my backyard in the bushes and trees.

Cardinals eat insects like worms, beetles and flies. Cardinals peck for seeds. A cardinal can fly and hop.

I like cardinals because they have masks. Cardinals are very alert!

Coco
By Vlad G.

The animal I chose to remember was my dog, Coco. Coco was a white dog that lived in my house when he was alive.

My dog ate meat and dog food. Coco did not play much because he was fat.

I liked Coco because he let me ride on his back.

Let's Discover ... Animals

Bailey
By Matt M.

The animal I chose to observe was a cat named Bailey. Bailey lives at Amanda's house. Amanda is my sister's friend.

Bailey moves low to the ground. Bailey eats food from PetSmart.

I like Bailey because he licks himself instead of taking a bath in a bathtub.

The Squirrel
By Ava P.

The animal I chose to observe was a squirrel. A few months ago, I found a lost baby squirrel and so I gave her milk and she came up with a milk mustache! I named her Martha.

Squirrels like Martha climb up my bird feeder and then go sliding down again like a fireman sliding down a pole. They eat acorns and nuts.

I like squirrels because they are cute, adorable, furry, small, very fast at scurrying and most of all, energetic!

By Mr. Flood's Falcons

Oscar
By Robbie W.

The animal I chose to observe was my fish named Oscar Williams. He likes to swim and he is so cute.

Oscar eats fish food. I give him a pinch of fish food each morning. He likes to swim.

I like Oscar because he likes me a lot. He is so cute. I like him a lot.

Raven
By Brian S.

The animal I chose to observe was my dog, Raven. Raven lives in a house.

Raven walks and eats bones. She runs around a lot.

I like pups like Raven because they're cute. My pup is fun to play with. She sleeps four hours a day. She likes the snow.

Let's Discover ... Animals

Cody
By Alex J.

The animal I chose to observe was my fish, Cody. He lives in a fish bowl with an anchor.

My fish swims and swims up to the surface to gobble up the fish flakes I feed him.

I like Cody because he looks at me when I look at him and he likes to play games like "Swim Around in a Circle" and "Tag My Tail." He's always playing that game.

Fritzy
By Neil C.

The animal I chose to remember was my dog, Fritzy. He lived in my house when he was alive. He was very frisky. I loved my dog Fritzy. He liked to play outside.

Fritzy ate dog food, biscuits, hot dogs, rice and apples. Fritzy only went on walks.

I liked my dog because he was very calm. He was also yappy.

By Mr. Katoen's Tigers 2

Cute Little Woodchuck
By Katrina K.

The animal I chose to observe was a woodchuck. My animal lives in the deep forest. His home is a burrow in the ground. I once saw one in a tree.

A woodchuck eats leafy plants and root veggies. It moves on four paws.

I like woodchucks because they are very rare. They are fat, fuzzy and brown. Their face is lighter than the rest of their bodies. Their hands are like gloves. They are so cute! A woodchuck is also known as a whistle pig or groundhog.

Jody
By Kathleen D.

The animal I chose to observe was Jody. Jody is my aunt's cat. She lives in my aunt's apartment. Jody likes to go under the bed and table.

Jody eats cat food such as Iams and Friskies. She eats crunchy chicken flavored Pounce treats, too. Jody chases teaser toys. She thinks they are mice. She scratched me twice. She sleeps in my Aunt Mary's bed.

I like Jody because she lets me pet her even though she scratched me. She has really soft fur. Jody is frisky and chubby. I like Jody.

Let's Discover ... Animals

My Cat Josie
By Jordan J.

The animal I chose to observe was my cat, Josie. She lives in my house. She likes to hide in closets. She also likes to hide in bags and suitcases.

Josie naps, purrs, meows, looks around, walks around the house, tries to scratch people and sometimes, she bites. Josie eats cat food and sometimes cat treats and grass. She gets her food from me and other members of my family. We put it in her bowl.

I like my cat Josie because she is soft, furry and cuddly. When Josie plays with string, she looks very cute. Josie is interesting when she plays with string.

Scruffy
By Rhett S.

The animal I chose to observe was my dog named Scruffy. Scruffy is an Australian cattle dog. This type of dog raises cattle on farms so it lives on a farm or in a house.

Scruffy eats kibble. He moves with his legs. Scruffy's favorite activity is chasing squirrels.

I like Scruffy because he is very funny and he loves to kiss me.

By Mr. Katoen's Tigers 2

The "Stealers"
By Gavin B.

The animal I chose to observe was a chipmunk. My animal lives in my backyard. Some chipmunks live in scrub areas and woodland.

Chipmunks steal bird eggs. They have huge pouches to carry their food. They run as fast as a hawk.

I like chipmunks because they are furry. Chipmunks are cute!

Gecky
By Miles R.

The animal I chose to observe was my pet gecko, Gecky. My gecko lives in a cage in my house.

My pet gecko crawls and it eats crickets and waxworms. I buy them at the pet store and feed them to her.

I like my gecko because she is fun to watch. My pet gecko is bumpyish and she has black spots.

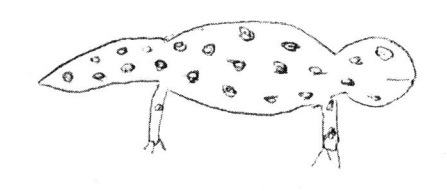

The Squirrel
By Phillip R.

The animal I chose to observe was a squirrel. The animal I picked makes a big nest out of twigs and leaves.

The squirrel climbs trees and eats berries, nuts and tomatoes. To get the nuts, it looks for them in the mulch.

I like squirrels because they are fun to chase and fun to watch dig in the ground.

Let's Discover ... Animals

Sven
By Dan T.

The animal I chose to observe was my cat, Sven. Sven bites like an ALLIGATOR! Once when I was a baby, I bit his tail. Sven lives in my house.

Sven eats leftover chicken and turkey from the table. He moves all around the house. Oh, and he eats cat food, too.

I love Sven. He's interesting because he will fight dogs because he's tougher than dogs.

My Neighbor's Dog
By Kaitlyn Y.

The animal I chose to observe was a dog. It is my neighbor's dog. It lives inside and outside.

My neighbor's dog moves on four legs. It likes dog food.

I like my neighbor's dog because it is playful.

By Mr. Katoen's Tigers 2

Abraham
By Chapin S.

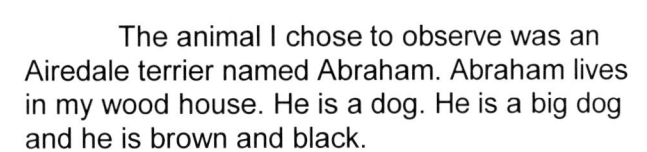

The animal I chose to observe was an Airedale terrier named Abraham. Abraham lives in my wood house. He is a dog. He is a big dog and he is brown and black.

My dog Abraham walks and he eats dog food. We put the food in a bowl. Abraham barely eats treats. He drinks water.

I like my dog Abraham because he is so nice. He is very interesting because he does not like to run like other dogs.

Horse
By Sam S.

The animal I chose to observe was a horse. The horse I observed lives in a field in Middleburg.

The horse runs and eats carrots, grass, hay and dung.

I like the horse because it nibbled on me. Horses are big and spectacular.

Let's Discover ... Animals

Why Woodpeckers Are Annoying
By Andrew B.

The animal I chose to observe was a woodpecker. My animal lives in a tree near Nottingham!

Woodpeckers move like this: they fly and move their beaks really, really quickly to get bugs in the trees.

I like woodpeckers because they are very "flighty." They are very cute. Woodpeckers are very "bird-brained." My animal is very annoying!

Zagara
By Arlo B.

The animal I chose to observe was my puppy, Zagara. Zagara is really funny. He gets into mischief. He lives in a crate. I love my puppy!

Zagara moves slinkily. He eats chicken and rice.

I like my puppy because he is sweet. I like to play fetch with my puppy. He is cool, too.

2009 © Nottingham Elementary School

By Mr. Katoen's Tigers 2

The Bluebird
By Patrick S.

The animal I chose to observe was a bluebird. Bluebirds live in nests in trees. Bluebirds fly to look for different homes. They sometimes live on the ground.

Bluebirds eat worms. They walk with their legs and they fly.

I like bluebirds because they are pretty and beautiful.

The Cutest Bunny
By Cate B.

The animal I chose to observe was a bunny. The bunny that I usually see a lot is in my backyard or in the bushes in our backyard. It is sometimes under our tree stump. The tree stump that the bunny goes under is really, really big.

The bunny moves by hopping or running away. The bunny eats a couple things such as carrots that we put outside. It can eat a lot of them. We have to feed carrots to the bunny. The bunny eats our grass that we grow because we have a ton of grass in our backyard.

I like the bunny I chose because it is extraordinarily cute. The bunny is chubby and it is very, very, very fuzzy and alert for foxes. The bunny is really precious. I think the bunny has extremely tall ears. I love the bunny!

Let's Discover ... Animals

A Cute Pig!
By Calla M.

The animal I chose to observe was a pig. She lives on a farm. She sleeps in a little barn.

The pig waddles and she likes to eat rotting carcasses. She also likes to eat grass and roots.

I like the pig because she is adorable, filthy and fat. I like my animal a lot.

Lucy
By Callie F.

The animal I chose to observe was Lucy, my neighbor's pet hound dog. Lucy lives in my neighbor's house and she plays outside. She rests in her crate.

Lucy runs, chews sticks and catches sticks. She is very excitable. Lucy is fun to watch. She eats dog food, biscuits and Frosty Paws ice cream for dogs. My neighbors give it to her.

I like Lucy because she is funny. She is amazing! She is fun to watch.

By Mr. Katoen's Tigers   2

A Dog Named Derby
By Gwen P.

The animal I chose to observe was my pet dog named Derby. She lives in my house and she sleeps in my sunroom. Derby likes to go outside in the backyard.

Derby eats dog food and sometimes steals table scraps. She scampers around searching for food. She likes to go on walks as well.

I like Derby because she is a cutie and she is very loving and caring. She is interesting to me because she does a lot of exciting things when I watch her.

Tucker
By Carly T.

The animal I chose to observe was my dog. His name is Tucker. He lives in my house. He sleeps on his cushion. That's mostly what he does.

I feed Tucker dog food and Milk Bones. Tucker is only three, but he doesn't move much.

I like my dog Tucker because he is clumsy, mellow and smart. I'll bet he is the clumsiest dog you've ever met.

Let's Discover ... Animals

Awesome Squirrels!
By Ryan K.

The animal I chose to observe was a squirrel. A squirrel lives in my backyard and the forest.

A squirrel climbs and skitters to get food. I often see it raiding our bird feeder. A squirrel mainly eats nuts and seeds.

I like squirrels because they're really fun to watch! They are very funny!

Deer
By Mikey C.

The animals I chose to observe were deer. They live in the woods. They stand still and are light brown, kind of soft and small.

Deer eat lots of plants and grass. They are quiet.

I like deer because they are nice.

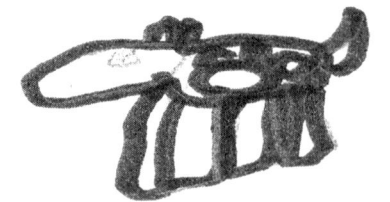

2009 © Nottingham Elementary School

By Mr. Katoen's Tigers

Snapping Turtles
By Alex S.

The animal I chose to observe was a snapping turtle. Snapping turtles live in streams, lakes, their shells and the Potomac River. Snapping turtles also live in mud.

The snapping turtle moves on its short, fat legs. It eats lizards, frogs, insects, snails, crayfish, river clams, algae, snakes, plants, toads, small fish, and other turtles.

I like the snapping turtle because it is awesome to watch. It looks really cool to see the snapping turtle in its natural habitat. There is moss covering the habitat so it makes it comfortable for the snapping turtle to sleep. The snapping turtle finds moss to sleep in at night. Some snapping turtles have soft shells. That's so cool. Some snapping turtles play in the mud. I think it looks so cool to see the snapping turtle sleep. I love snapping turtles!

The Deer Is...
By Sophia R.

The animal I chose to observe was a deer. This animal is usually located in a park, woods or on the plain.

My animal travels by foot and it eats grass and sometimes leaves.

I like that deer are loving, shy animals except when it comes to protecting their babies. I also like that their babies are safe with them and they are very, very cute. I think it's awesome that when they are fawns, they have spots and when they are grown-ups they don't. The males, when they are fawns, don't have any horns but when they grow up, they do. Cool! I love deer!

Let's Discover ... Animals

The Parakeet
By Della H.

The animal I chose to observe was a parakeet. It lives in my neighbor's house in a cage. He loves carrots and birdseed. He is really scared of everybody that is why I call him Scaredy Cat Bird. He had a brother, but he died. There is another bird who lives in the cage next to him whose name is Ralph.

Scaredy Cat Bird flies around inside, but sometimes he walks and he does not eat much. But when he does eat, he eats carrots and birdseed.

I like my neighbor's parakeet because he is very cute and he does not bite. He has really pretty feathers. The colors of his feathers are yellow and green.

My Dog
By Favio A.

The animal I chose to observe is Coco, my dog. Coco lives in my house in a cage. He lays on these two blankets next to my other dog, Oreo. It seems like Coco is stronger than my other dog who is older.

Coco chases squirrels outside. Coco eats Priority dog food, dog treats, and water. Coco scratches the door when he wants to go outside.

I like Coco because he is puffy so I can be warm when I'm cold. He looks like snow. Of course, he is white. He likes to play in the backyard. I think he is the smartest dog in the world.

By Mrs. Stegall's Seagulls

My All Red Fish
By Jack M.

The animal I chose to observe was my fish. He lives in a plastic tank in my living room. I feed him fish food. He is my longest living fish.

My fish gets around by swimming. He eats fish food.

I like my fish because it is fun to watch him eat. He has red scales and red fins. I love my fish!

The Squirrel
By Jared W.

The animal I chose to observe was a squirrel. I see squirrels everywhere. They live in nests in trees. Squirrels are small with fuzzy tails. Squirrels have gray, brown, reddish or black fur.

Squirrels run, jump and climb trees. They eat nuts, pumpkins and berries. They find their food on the ground.

I like squirrels because they are fuzzy. Squirrels like to play a lot.

I Love Birds
By Caroline B.

The animal I chose to observe was a bird. Birds live in nests. The nests are in bushes and trees. Birds like to sing pretty songs. Birds are very pretty! They can be red, orange, yellow, green, blue, purple, pink, brown, black and gray. Maybe?

Birds get around by flying. Birds eat worms, big worms. Birds also like to eat the birdseed people put out, but sometimes the squirrels eat the birdseed. Birds can also get around by walking but usually, they get scared.

I like birds because they can be different colors and they are pretty! Birds sing lovely songs and they are interesting and unique! Birds are awesome!

125 2009 © Nottingham Elementary School

Let's Discover ... Animals

Matey
By Luke W.

The animal I chose to observe was my cat, Matey. He lives everywhere in my house ... in my basement, upper level and lower level, but not my attic.

Matey walks on four small-sized paws. He eats cat food. Matey never catches any mice.

I like Matey because he is fun to watch. He is very soft. He is only ten years old and that is only 15 years in cat style.

Pele
By Cole W.

The animal I chose to observe was my dog, Pele. Pele lives in my house and she sleeps under my mom and dad's bed. Sometimes she sleeps on my brother's bed.

My dog Pele likes to chase squirrels and birds. She steals food from us and eats dog food.

I like my dog Pele because she is very fun to play with. She is really soft and furry. Pele barks when she sees other people. I think Pele is the best dog in the world!

By Mrs. Stegall's Seagulls

The Tale of Schatzie
By Chuck W.

The animal I chose to observe was my dog, Schatzie. My dog lives in a cage in my basement. The cage she lives in has a cushion in the middle and bars for the rest.

Schatzie loves bones! But mostly, she eats dog food. Schatzie moves by feet … four feet… four medium/large feet that are brown.

I like my dog Schatzie because she barks cool and begs for food. In order to get food, Schatzie also loves to kiss or lick! However you like it, Schatzie is very nice and I think she is the best dog in the world!

The Tale of … Tiger
By Elizabeth L.

The animal I chose to observe was my cat, Tiger. Her nicknames are Tig Tiggy and Tige. Tiger is two years old. Her birthday is May 13th. She was born in Reston. There is one annoying thing about her … she's an alarm clock with … NO OFF BUTTON! Every morning, "Meow! Meow! Meow!" on and on and on!

Tiger is a bug killer. Here's how she does it: 1 … pounce. 2 … kill. 3 … play. 4 … is the gross part. 4 … EAT! So eating the bugs = sick kitten in 30 or so minutes. When Tiger was thin, she had a secret passage behind the toilet. Tiger loves to watch birds, people, squirrels and leaves. When it rains, leaves stick to the window so she bats at the leaves. In the summer, moths tease Tiger. They'll stick to the window and won't move.

Tiger is allowed to go outside as long as someone holds her. When Tiger was a kitten, she would not eat her kitten food so Louie ate hers and she ate his. Tiger is warm and flexible. She is the best cat ever!

Let's Discover ... Animals

The Real Adventures of Bingo
By Seth G.

The animal I chose to observe was my dog, Bingo. She is ten years old. She lives in my house. She sleeps by the PS2. I love her so much.

Bingo walks slowly. She eats dog food. She had a leg problem for a couple of years.

I like to sleep on Bingo because she is warm. She is very sweet. She is sooooooo cute. She is the best dog in the world!

Red
By Cass Y.

The animal I chose to observe was a red squirrel. Red squirrels live in my neighborhood, in forests and in trees. They sleep in trees, too.

Red squirrels climb, hide and stare or they may not notice when I observe them. They eat acorns, hickory nuts, beech nuts, hazelnuts, butternuts and berries.

I like red squirrels because they like to skitter and scatter all the time. Plus, it seems like they like to play hide-and-seek and tag in the trees, too. I also like them because they get scared and run away when they notice me.

By Mrs. Stegall's Seagulls 2

Harly, My Dog
By John Thomas D.

The animal I chose to observe was my dog, Harly. Harly lives in our house where he sleeps all day long. Harly sleeps under a bed and on a bed but that rarely happens because my parents tell him to get off.

My animal moves on four paws. Harly eats dog food but we have to go to Harris Teeter to get his food. Harly does drink water. Harly eats artificial bacon and sometimes has bones ... usually one time each day.

I like Harly. He is so nice because he never gets angry at you. Harly also lets me lay on him, but not too long because it kind of hurts him. Harly is so furry and has really smooth fur. Harly does not like any kind of tape at all. I'm so glad he's my dog.

My Hamster Daisy
By Alex M.

My hamster Daisy lives in a cage and sleeps on cotton.

My hamster Daisy eats apples, hamster food, green food, seeds, carrots, strawberries, grapes, pumpkin seeds, tomatoes and peppers.

I like Daisy because she is soft, fluffy and fuzzy. She is black and has black eyes and a stubby tail. She is fat and looks like a big fluff ball!!!!! She also looks like a miniature black bear. I think my hamster is the ... best!!!!!!

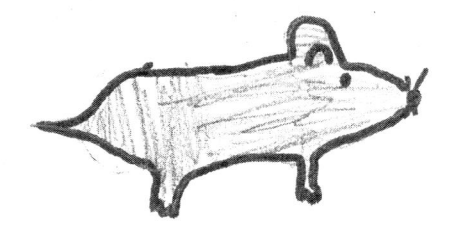

Let's Discover ... Animals

All About My Dog
By Josh J.

The animal I chose to observe was my dog, Skylar. She lives in my house. She sleeps in her metal cage.

Skylar walks and eats dog food. She also eats our plants and that makes my mom mad!

I like my dog Skylar because she is an awesome dog. I like my dog Skylar a lot. She listens when I ask her to do something.

Zeppelin
By Alecia S.

My dog Zeppelin lives in my house. He sleeps next to me on the floor. My dog has toys and a big bone.

My dog Zeppelin runs and walks around the yard. He eats dry and wet dog food. Zeppelin has to work for his treats.

I like Zeppelin because he is fun to play with. I think he may be the best dog in the world! Yeah, that's what I think.

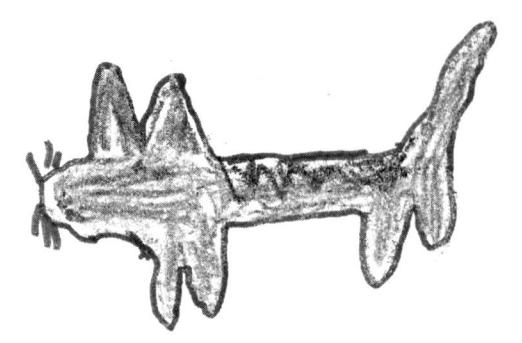

By Mrs. Stegall's Seagulls

Dogs
By Louisa C.

The animal I chose to observe was a dog. Wild dogs run in groups. Their babies are called puppies. Dogs play a lot. They have very sharp teeth. They grow to be strong and big. Dogs can hear from far away. They can run fast.

Dogs move on four legs. They eat meat and crumbs when they drop on the floor. They are really good vacuum cleaners. They jump all the time. They often take walks. Dogs play fetch a lot in the backyard.

I like dogs because they are so cute, cuddly and playful. They are fuzzy and warm. They love me and I love them.

Birds
By Audrey G.

The animal I chose to observe was a bird. The bird I observed lives in my big backyard. Birds also live up in trees in nests.

A bird uses its wings to fly up into the sky and go to the destination of its choice. A bird eats many things like berries, worms and nuts. Birds flap their wings and hop like little tiny crickets.

I like birds because they are very pretty and cute. Birds fly with their wings. I really do love birds.

Let's Discover ... Animals

All About Ducklings
By Marina G.

The animal I chose to observe was a duckling. It lives in a nest when it is still a baby. The duckling's nest is usually near a lake, river, pond or stream. If it rains, the duckling might even paddle in a puddle.

A duckling moves by paddling around. The way it catches food is by diving. Its favorite food is plump fish. Ducklings also eat reeds and bugs.

I like ducklings because they are fluffy and very tiny. Their eyes make them look like they are guilty of something. I think ducklings are awesome!

My Dog Mandy
By John M.

The animal I chose to observe was my pet dog, Mandy. She lives in my house. She sleeps on my mom's bed. Mandy loves my mom.

Mandy runs and walks. Mandy eats dog food with this slimy stuff. She gets her food because my mom feeds her.

I like Mandy because she is my pet. I like to lie down with her. She is interesting to me because she is very shy.

By Mrs. Stegall's Seagulls

Quincy the Puppy
By Mary W.

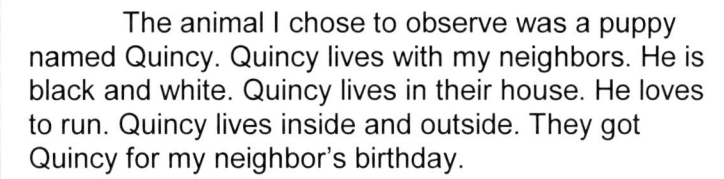

The animal I chose to observe was a puppy named Quincy. Quincy lives with my neighbors. He is black and white. Quincy lives in their house. He loves to run. Quincy lives inside and outside. They got Quincy for my neighbor's birthday.

Quincy plays, chews, licks, sniffs, sits and shakes. They feed Quincy dog food and treats. My neighbors give it to him. Quincy drinks water.

I like Quincy because he is so cute! Quincy is very small. Quincy is a very cool breed. He's a puppy so he is very active. Quincy has a trainer. Quincy grows a little bit. They take really good care of him.

Mimi, Mimi, Mimi
By Olivia E.

The animal I chose to observe was my dog, Mimi. Mimi eats dog food and lives in my home. Sometimes, Mimi has to go to the vet. Mimi does not like the vet so we have to give her a dog treat when we get home.

Mimi's favorite game is Tug. Mimi's favorite toy is her stuffed squirrel. I like Mimi because she is small and soft.

I like Mimi, my dog, because she is small, soft and cuddly. Mimi is also funny sometimes. If there is a dog toy on your head, Mimi will climb on your lap and get it down. When Mimi licks you, it tickles. Mimi is a wonderful dog.

Let's Discover ... Animals

The Neighborhood Cat
By John Riley B.

The animal I chose to observe was a cat. I decided to do the neighborhood cat because I don't have a pet yet. The cat's name is Malcolm. In the winter, he comes in by the fire to warm up. He is also very playful.

Malcolm walks very quietly. When he's not playing, he's chasing mice and other small rodents. Malcolm eats cat food, birds, mice, rats, badgers, groundhogs, moles and occasionally, bugs and garden snakes. He doesn't have big paws, but he can walk on the fence with them.

I like that Malcolm is helpful because if a squirrel gets in anybody's birdfeeder, he'll pounce on them. One time when a kid was bullying my sister, Malcolm jumped up and attacked the bully. Malcolm is the best cat in the world!

The Smart Deer
By Ellie T.

The animal I chose to observe was a deer. Deer live in the wild because they are not pets. However, they do not look like wild animals because they look like they would like you.

Deer eat vegetables, plants and leaves. When they hear danger or something else, they stop eating, stand straight, pause and listen very carefully. When the noise stops, they go back to eating. They get vegetables from people's gardens.

I like deer because they are very gentle. A deer is a pretty animal and it is brown. I like the color brown. I chose a deer because they walk around my neighborhood. They are also hard to see. I don't know if you have ever seen a deer with antlers. That is a male deer. I have seen one. I hope you see one soon.

By Mrs. Stegall's Seagulls

Truffles
By Ethan S.

The animal I chose to observe was a rabbit. Its name is Truffles. Truffles is a big fluff ball.

Truffles hops. He eats pellets, cabbage and hay. Truffles' weekly allowance is a carrot.

I like Truffles because he's a big fluff ball. His birthday is November 3rd. When you take him out, he tries to climb the hutch roof. Truffles is cute.

The Unnamed Fish For Three Years
By Benjamin G.

The animal I chose to observe was a fish named Teddy! My fish Teddy lives in a fish bowl. He is a guppy. We got Teddy three years ago. He is old for a fish.

Teddy eats fish food. He wiggles to swim. Teddy swims to his food.

I like Teddy because he is interesting and he is transparent. He is different colors like orange and silver on his body. Teddy has blue eyes and red lines. Teddy floats around. Teddy has little fins. I like watching Teddy.

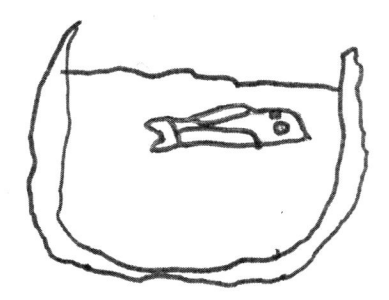

Let's Discover ... Animals

Ginger
By Josh F.

The animal I chose to observe was my dog. Her name is Ginger. She is a Chowhound. Most of the time, Ginger lives in the house.

My dog eats dog food. Usually my dad feeds her. Ginger is fourteen and she is slow. When you touch her, she jumps. She slips on ice in winter.

I like Ginger because she is part of my family. She likes to go outside. I hug Ginger a lot. Ginger is a great dog.

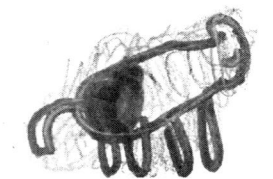

Cool Squirrels
By Nathan B.

The animal I chose to observe was a squirrel. It lives in the backyard in a big oak tree.

The squirrel runs very, very fast and eats nuts.

I like squirrels because they are cool.

By Mrs. Way's Wise Owls

2

Squirrels Rule
By Jackson S.

The animal I chose to observe was a squirrel. My animal lives outside. It lives in a tree. It has a nest in the hollow of the tree.

My animal eats nuts, acorns and berries. It hunts its food. My animal runs fast.

Squirrels like to climb up trees. They are fun to watch. They are hyper. They start and stop. They have twitchy movements. I like squirrels.

My Dog Pepper
By Jamie R.

The animal I chose to observe was my dog, Pepper. Pepper lives on the middle floor of my house. She has really, really soft hair. She chews up almost anything she sees. I think she is a mix between a German shepherd and a black lab.

My dog moves by walking and crawling. My mom and dad feed her dog food and a little bit of meat.

I like my dog, Pepper because she is very soft. She also licks A LOT! Some of the time, she is very calm. She loves when I throw her toys.

Let's Discover ... Animals

Squirrels
By Micah G.

The animal I chose to observe was a squirrel. Squirrels come out in the spring. They live in trees in my backyard.

My animal scurries, runs and climbs. Squirrels eat acorns and tomatoes.

I like squirrels because they are so cute and fluffy. Squirrels are interesting to me because they are fun to watch. I like squirrels.

Biscuit
By Garrett F.

The animal I chose to observe was my dog, Biscuit. She is a guard dog and a yellow lab. She lives in my house.

My dog Biscuit does not move much. She is very old. She gets a lot of food by begging.

I like Biscuit because she is cute and cuddly. I love Biscuit!

Jessie
By Alexander B.

The animal I chose to observe was a dog. She lives in my house. Her name is Jessie.

Jessie runs and walks. She eats dog food. She eats people food, too.

I like my dog because she is loyal and smart. Dogs are good animals.

By Mrs. Way's Wise Owls

A Soft Animal
By Midge C.

The animal I chose to observe was a kitten. My kitten lives in my house. My kitten's name is Goldee.

Goldee is always pouncing on things. Goldee eats salmon and cat food. I always have to feed her. She is very sneaky and quiet.

I like Goldee because she is very cuddly. I call my kitten Goldee because she is gold and yellow, too. She is also very small and soft.

My Chipmunk Stripey
By Jonathan V.

The animal I chose to observe was a chipmunk, Stripey. He lives in my backyard.

Stripey loves to play tag with his brothers. He loves to scamper around my backyard. He loves to eat nuts.

I like Stripey because he is very, very, very fast! He sometimes scampers to me. He races his brothers. He is fun to hang around with.

Let's Discover ... Animals

Maggie
By Will C.

The animal I chose to observe was my cousin's golden retriever, Maggie. Maggie lives in Springfield, Virginia in a cul de sac.

Maggie walks. When she walks, she wags her tail. She barks when people come into the house. She runs fast when she wants to lick you. Maggie eats dog food. She loves to eat steak.

I like Maggie because she is soft, silky and furry. She also likes to be hugged. I really like Maggie because I like dogs!

Sick Fox
By Alex K.

The animal I chose to observe was a fox. One fall day, I saw a fox in my backyard. It was sick.

The sick fox did absolutely nothing at all. Normally, foxes eat other animals and berries.

I liked the fox because it was fun to watch. It was interesting because it was sick.

By Mrs. Way's Wise Owls   2

The Penguins of the World
By Liam E.

The animal I chose to observe was a penguin. Penguins live in four places: Antarctica, Penguin Park, Chile and the oceans.

My animal waddles and swims to get places. Penguins swim really fast. Penguins eat fish and krill. They also slide.

I like penguins because they look cute and cuddly. I like penguins because of how they waddle. It's funny sometimes. It's cute how they start to slide. I love penguins.

The Cat
By Isabelle H.

The animal I chose to observe was a cat. It goes to other houses in the neighborhood when we are walking. The cat is gray. It crawls on the ground and when it goes outside, it finds birds.

My cat moves on four legs. It eats cat food. Everyone in the family feeds the cat.

I like cats because they run a lot and chase strings. They also play with me.

Let's Discover ... Animals

Frogs
By Michael G.

The animal I chose to observe was a frog. Frogs live in ponds, creeks, swamps, lakes and rivers. In forests, frogs live in mud piles.

Frogs eat flies and insects. They catch them by sticking their tongues out. Frogs move by hopping and swimming.

I like frogs because they hop around a lot. They croak a lot. Frogs sit there half the time. I like frogs because they are fast and have shiny skin. Frogs are really cool.

My Furry Squirrel
By Caroline P.

The animal I chose to observe was a furry squirrel. The squirrel lives outside in my backyard in a nest. The nest is in a tree.

My animal moves by scurrying. The squirrel eats peanuts. He runs up the fence and gets peanuts from my neighbor's peanut feeder. He throws the shells in my yard.

I like my furry squirrel because it plays, scurries and wrestles. It is interesting because it goes on the monkey bars and down the slide. I love my squirrel!

By Mrs. Way's Wise Owls 2

Lauren's Dog, Stone
By Zoe C.

The animal I chose to observe was my friend Lauren's dog named Stone. He lives in Lauren's house and backyard. He is a very good dog.

Stone does not run. He barely jumps and walks. Stone eats dog food called Purina One and dog treats. Stone drinks water.

I like Stone because he is very friendly and doesn't jump on people. I like dogs because they are cuddly and cute. The reason I chose a dog is because dogs make good pets.

Birds
By Ethan W.

The animals I chose to observe were birds. The birds live in nests in trees and in holly bushes in my yard.

Birds fly, hop and look for food. They eat worms, berries and birdseed. They dig for food in the woods and meadows.

I like birds because they are plump, cute, colorful, soft and chirpy. They can fly and we cannot. I like birds.

2009 © Nottingham Elementary School

Let's Discover ... Animals

Goldie
By Meghan D.

The animal I chose to observe was a fish. My animal lives in my house. She is a Beta fish. Her name is Goldie. She lives in a very nice tank. Over the tank, there is a pretty container that has flowers over it.

Goldie eats the food we give her. The food we give her looks like very small balls. She moves by wiggling her tail.

I like my pet because she has two colors. The colors are blue and red. She is very shy. She usually hides in the back of the tank. I love Goldie.

Sophie
By Anabel B.

The animal I chose to observe was my dog, Sophie. She lives in my house. Sophie is a Great Dane. We adopted her from another family.

Sophie eats cheese, chicken and kibble. Of course, she walks and sometimes she runs.

I like my dog Sophie because she likes to snuggle. She is interesting because she likes cats.

By Mrs. Way's Wise Owls

2

Fish
By Emily S.

The animal I chose to observe was a fish that likes to swim. Some fish live in aquariums in tanks made of glass. At the bottom of the tank, there are usually different colored marbles or rocks. On top of the marbles are usually big fake rocks with tunnels. Sometimes the rocks are real, but rarely.

All fish like to swim. All fish move their tails in a side-to-side movement. It is fun to watch. Some fish eat fish food. If you drop fish food in the tank, the fish swim to the food, hesitate and eat it.

I like fish because they can breathe in water, not in air. That's really cool. They can swim their whole lives. They can do whatever they would like to do! I think being a fish would be fun but dangerous. I like petting fish when I get to pet them. I think fish are fishy, cute and scaly. Fish are interesting.

What My Animal Does
By Ava F.

The animal I chose to observe was an owl that is nocturnal and stays up at night. The owl sleeps in the day. My animal lives in the woods by my house and I can hear it every night.

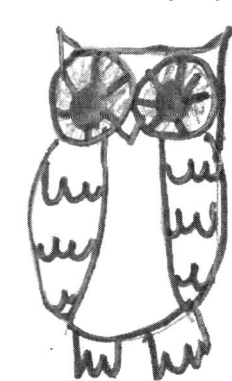

My animal moves by flapping its wings up and down. It eats mice down by the woods or where there are a lot of trees.

I like my owl friend because it is a colorful owl and it is a funny owl and a cool one. He always goes close to my house and makes his hoots kind of funny like this, "Hoot, hoot, hoot!"

Let's Discover ... Animals

My Sven
By Emma T.

The animal I chose to observe was my cat, Sven. His habitat is my house. When I watch my cat, he leaps, jumps, runs, plays, lays down, chases and EATS! Speaking of eating, he loves chicken.

Sven eats cat food. My family calls it wet food and dry food. My cat walks, jumps, runs and sneaks on all fours.

I like my cat Sven because he is cuddly and fun to have around. Sven is interesting because he is smart, flexible, big and muscular. I love my Svenypoo!

Squirrel
By Alaina E.

The animal I chose to observe was a squirrel. It lives in a hollow hole in a tree and it visits the woods. It is hungry. Sometimes I hold nuts for it.

The squirrel scurries up trees. It picks up nuts and eats the herbs in our herb garden.

I like the squirrel. I named her Amanda. I like the squirrel because she has a fluffy tail and a furry body. I like the way the squirrel follows me, too. I like to feed her nuts when I go on walks.

By Mrs. Way's Wise Owls 2

My Cats
By Hank F.

The animals I chose to observe were cats. My cats live in my home. They are indoor cats. Their names are Gussy, Lucy and Stella.

My cats walk around the house. They eat cat food. My mom feeds the cats.

I like my cats because they come when I call them. They are interesting because of their colors … gold and white. They spend time with me. I love my cats.

My Pet
By Sawyer M.

The animal I chose to observe was my parrot. My parrot lives in a cage in my house. Her name is Cinderella. My parrot has a bell and a bridge in her cage.

My parrot climbs on her bell. We feed her crackers.

I like Cinderella because she is colorful and fun. Parrots make lots of noise. Cinderella is the greatest!

My Incredible Imagination ... Inventions

The Amazing Thing
By Ann M.

My invention is called the Amazing Thing. The Amazing Thing does whatever you want it to do.

The Amazing Thing is purple and black. It wears the coolest clothes. It is about four feet tall. The Amazing Thing says almost anything. When you clap eight times, the Amazing Thing comes to you. For example, if you want to buy an iPod, it will buy an iPod for you.

I'm going to sell The Amazing Thing all around the world. The Amazing Thing will cost $9,888 because it takes a long time to make and train. A boy named Bob bought one for his sister, Selena, for her birthday. Lots of other people bought it, too!

The Breakfast Maker
By Tate R.

My invention is called the Breakfast Maker. It makes breakfast for people who can be a little lazy.

My Breakfast Maker works on solar power. The invention can be big or small and it has a computer in it. The Breakfast Maker can make anything, even pizza! The invention has buttons you press that show your choices. When you press the buttons, it gives it to you.

You can buy The Breakfast Maker for $400.00. You can buy it anywhere but the store with the most Breakfast Makers is LA-LA –LAND! This is in stores TODAY! Everybody is buying it now.

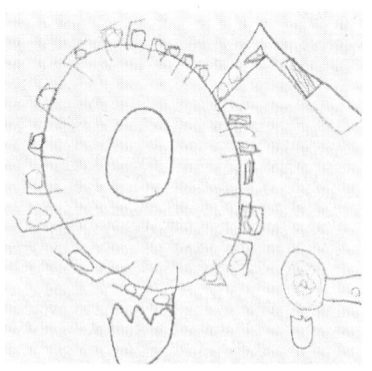

By Mrs. Gorham/Lamb's Hall of Famers

3

The Amazing Invisible Projector
By Brian G.

My invention is called the Amazing Invisible Projector. It projects an image of you, and the projection does everything you would do.

The Amazing Invisible Projector is small, camouflaged to its surroundings and is made of metal. You only have to press a single button and POW! There you have it! Say you were at school, you pop it out and sneak it somewhere in the classroom; then you pretend to go to the bathroom and sneak out of school!

The Amazing Invisible Projector costs $159.99. You can buy it at Target, Radio Shack, Toys 'R Us and Wal-Mart. Children would probably be the only people who would want to buy it and maybe adults.

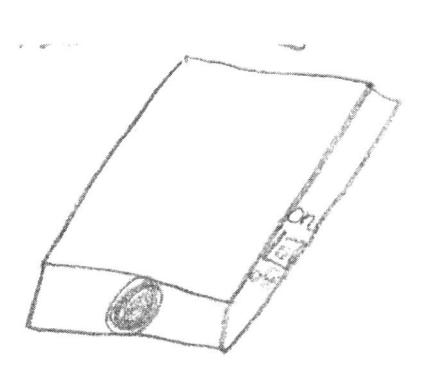

Mini Computer
By Peyton K.

My invention is called Mini Computer. It does everything a perfect computer does.

The Mini Computer looks like a small computer, but better. It will copy everything you say into the small microphone. After you speak into the small microphone, it will print out everything you say on the screen. The Mini Computer works on two things, electricity and small batteries.

The Mini Computer will sell at Best Buy and Target. It will cost $199.99. People who are small would like to buy it, as well as people who do not like to carry things.

2009 © Nottingham Elementary School

My Incredible Imagination ... Inventions

Q2-A7
By Enrique D.

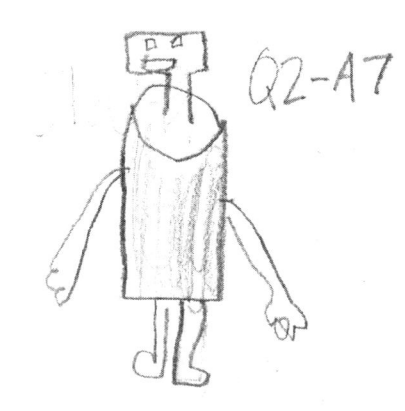

My invention is a robot. Its name is Q2-A7. It can speak every language. It can also speak alien and animal languages.

Q2-A7 comes in silver, blue and red. You can turn it on on the bottom of the stomach. It has a square head. To talk to it, you have to speak into a tiny microphone that clips to your clothes. So if you say, "Run!", Q2-A7 will run.

Q2-A7 will cost $120.

The ?
By Owen G.

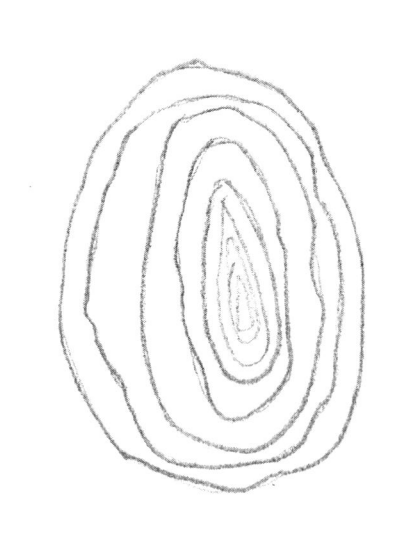

My invention is called the ?. It makes anything appear ... toys, books, ANYTHING! P.S. It also includes food, homework and much, much more.

The ? looks like a target but it's all purple with white rings. It is powered by magic, and it makes absolutely no sound. P.S. You have to have a wand/staff to own it.

I will give the ? away once every 50 years in the middle of the forest. Only wizards and witches can buy it. P.S. The last one will cost $1,000,000 in cash.

By Mrs. Gorham/Lamb's Hall of Famers

The Telepathic Fantasy Door
By Frank L.

The Telepathic Fantasy Door will eliminate rainy day boredom forever. It is a machine that taps into a person's memory and projects that image in the door. It will turn on for you. It is quiet and it doesn't smell. A mouse can't even hear it when it's on.

The Telepathic Fantasy Door is powered by solar, wind and enjoyment. It is cheap, made of metal, medium-sized, and it's customized. It is cheap to repair, is indestructible, shiny, waterproof, mobile, lightweight and high-tech.

The price is a mere $10 and it has a ten year guarantee. You can make it real with a Make Real button installed on it. Every kid will want one. It's also good for educational use. You can buy it at any local store. It's a great source of fun!

The Tell-a-Bot
By Ian D.

My invention is called the Tell-a-Bot. I called it the Tell-a-Bot because when you tell the Tell-a-Bot something, it will give it to you.

The Tell-a-Bot is made out of steel. The Tell-a-Bot runs on solar power or electricity. Inside its body there is a computer.

My Tell-a-Bot will sell for $100. I will sell my Tell-a-Bot at Target and on Ebay. I think kids who have too much work to do will buy it.

My Incredible Imagination ... Inventions

THE PS-HERE-BOT
By Nick P.

The PS-HERE-BOT is a telepathic, smart, indestructible, shift-shaper, that is rich, great, cool and the best. The PS-HERE-BOT reads minds.

The PS-HERE-BOT will shift shape when someone mean is coming and it will trap the person. The PS-HERE-BOT is medium-sized and sometimes quiet. It is playful and nice. The PS-HERE-BOT will make sounds when you want it to. It is controlled by a remote that says, "Power." It has wheels and a microwave, too. The PS-HERE-BOT is also found in England. When you are playing hide-and-seek, it sprays camouflage gas on you so they can't find you. It has a built-in camera that takes pictures and it also comes to life. It has a built-in workshop, a Target store and a mall inside it. It has a mini little robot inside of it, too.

The PS-HERE-BOT is something all kids need. It will help grownups around the house, too. It is powered by air and sports. This is only available in stores. It cost $310.

The Hologram Maker
By Jasmin C.

The Hologram Maker works with batteries and it is made out of metal. It can hologram anything in the world.

The Hologram Maker can hologram a dog. It can even hologram a hologram! It can turn a hologram to life. If you don't want to go to school, you can hologram yourself. It also can turn an apple into a block.

The Hologram Maker costs $5,000. I will use it because then I won't have to go to Ross when I'm tired.

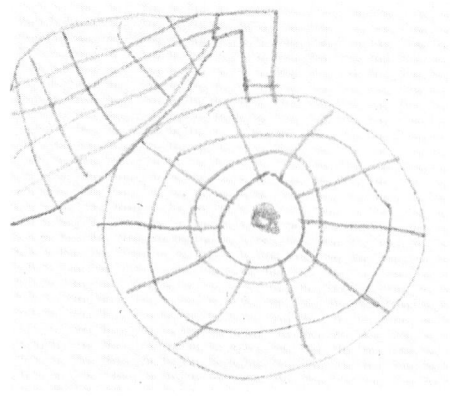

By Mrs. Gorham/Lamb's Hall of Famers

The Wish~A~Bot
By Gabrielle S.

The name of my robot is Wish~A~Bot. A Wish~A~Bot can give you anything you want.

The Wish~A~Bot is made of light, shiny metal. All the buttons are bright and shiny red except for the "on" button. It is bright green and big. The Wish~A~Bot talks like this, "Hello, what is your wish?" and then you say what your wish is. On top of its head it has a gold antenna. The Wish~A~Bot looks for the item you want, then drops it out. The Wish~A~Bot runs on solar power and it has a G.P.S. It does not make a peep.

Boys and girls all over the world will buy it. The Wish~A~Bot will cost $30. You can get it at this number: 555-555-5555.

The Movie Man
By Nate B.

My invention is The Movie Man. It can take you back in time or put you in a movie.

The Movie Man looks like a T.V. person with four hands and a regular body. It does not make any sound. My invention works with batteries which never run out.

I will sell the Movie Man in Canada and it will cost $10,000,000. Everyone will want to buy it.

My Incredible Imagination ... Inventions

Mr. School
By Nathalie B.

My Invention is called Mr. School. It can do anything for me, like make dinner or bake a cake.

Mr. School can do school work. It can take my spot when I don't want to go to school. It can get me dressed, undressed, and it can do my homework and schoolwork. Mr. School looks like this (see picture). It eats metal and it has hands and legs. My robot makes sounds and talks.

Mr. School costs $900. He is for everyone. If someone bought my robot, I would spend the $900 on more things to make another robot. But if I sold two, I would spend the money on holiday gifts for my family and myself.

By Mrs. Gorham/Lamb's Hall of Famers

The Homework Machine
By Lincoln K.

The name of my invention is the Homework Machine. It does your homework. Well, not just your homework ... any work for you.

My Homework Machine looks like a small machine you'd see in a factory. It has a short tube that you put any work in. Then you walk to the bucket and wait for it to come out. It has a robot that does your homework, a checker box checks the work and then you take it to school. It is made out of gold and silver. It is cool because it never runs out. It is very helpful because I never have to do any work. It is not just cool. It is awesome because it never breaks! It can go anywhere. It is tiny.

The Homework Machine cost $100,000.99. I will sell it at ???????? (You have to guess!)

The Break Worker
By Mark C.

My Invention is called the Break Worker. It makes your breakfast and does your homework. You say what you want and the Break Worker does it.

The Break Worker is amazing!!! If you want the Break Worker to do your homework, you put it in the slot and it does it! In the morning, it's ready! It makes a funny noise. All it says is "Beep!" It is a square.

The Break Worker costs $1 million. You can buy it at Wal-Mart. Kids will probably buy it for their homework.

My Incredible Imagination ... Inventions

Working Person
By Meghan H.

My invention is called Working Person. My invention is a girl. She will do anything I tell her to do. She will do my work, go to school for me and then come home to teach me everything she learned .

My Working Person looks like me so she can go to school for me. She's made out of metal and doesn't make any sounds unless she is speaking or is rusty. My Working Person is INDESTRUCTIBLE unless she gets shot in the heart. She is four feet tall and grows like I do. My Working Person runs on food and sugar. As you can see, she can wear clothes and eat food just like me.

I want to sell the Working Person at Springfield Mall and Ballston Mall. I will sell her for $2,000 or less. I hope you buy my invention.

The Paris Transportation Robot
By Olivia E.

My invention is called the Paris Transportation Robot. The Paris Transportation Robot is really rich. It can buy you anything you want in Paris! You just pick out the clothes you want and the Paris Transportation Robot buys them for you.

The Paris Transportation Robot is made out of metal and is painted blue and purple. It is so small it can fit in your pocket. It does not make any sounds. Whenever you snap your fingers, the Paris Transportation Robot takes you to Paris. You and the robot go really fast without having to wait to ask your parents.

The Paris Transportation Robot sells at gift shops in airports. It costs $8,888 because it takes about six months to make, so we have a lot of people on the job. I think a lot of kids and teenagers will buy it because they love to shop.

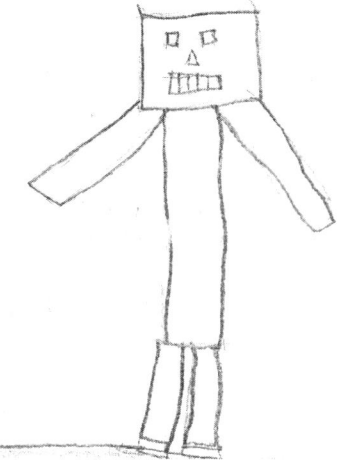

By Mrs. Gorham/Lamb's Hall of Famers

Hovercar
By Ryan J.

My invention is a Hovercar. My Hovercar does a huge amount of things.

One thing my Hovercar does … it drives for you so you can watch a movie on the windshield! It also has a lot of space in it. Your seat can turn around and you can work! It also has a tray to eat on. A radio (any kind) can be installed. When the Hovercar is parked, it has a stabilizer so it pushes the car up off the ground. The Hovercar is a car, but it doesn't look like one. It looks like a taxi that's floating in mid-air. Inside, it has seats in the middle, shelves and a projector in the back and a radio and tray in the front. The Hovercar is silent, so if it starts making noise, repair it! The Hovercar works by opening a hatch and inserting eight AAA, AA, C or D batteries inside. The batteries wear out in about two months, so you don't need to change them often.

If you want this invention, go to any Toyota or Ford dealership or any car shop, unless it is a used car rental. You will pay $479.99 for the Hovercar. This is going to be a very popular seller, and everyone will want to buy it! So, if you like hovering things and cars, come get the Hovercar for $479.99!!

My Incredible Imagination ... Inventions

The Amazing 4-D Copier
By Garrett L.

The name of my invention is the Amazing 4-D Copier. If you want something alive, you print a piece of paper of it and put it in the 4-D Copier and then it becomes alive.

My 4-D Copier looks like a regular copier but it is a little smaller. It's made out of fiberglass. It sounds like a regular printer but softer. My invention runs on solar power. There are a bunch of wheels inside that turn the paper around under bright lights which makes the thing come out of the paper.

I'm going to sell my invention at electronic stores in North America, Asia, and Europe. My invention will cost $600.99. If you buy it the day it comes out, then it will cost $200.60. Anybody can buy the 4-D Copier if they want it. I think it will be a humongous hit!!!

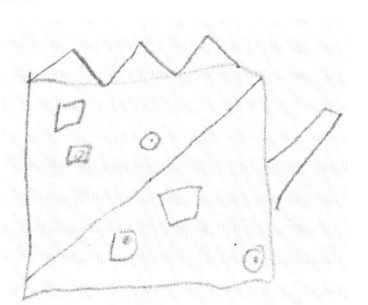

The Amazing Flyer
By Dina L.

My invention name is the Amazing Flyer because it flies. My invention helps the environment. When you get cold, it will give you a coat. When it is raining and there's lightning, it keeps it away.

My invention looks like a big doll but without any feet. It is made of metal. My invention only talks back but does not make any more sound. If you want it to go to a place, just tell it and it will take you there. My invention needs no gas. All it needs is someone to tell it where to go.

I am going to sell the Amazing Flyer at CVS and places where they sell sports stuff and car stores. If you want to buy my invention it will cost your age, but if you are 50 years or older it will cost $50. If you are a teen and younger, you have to have a parent with you.

By Mr. Knott's Bulldogs

3

The Futureless
By Mary S.

My invention is called Futureless. It will show you the future! It is super powerful, so it will send ideas to your brain. It will be the real future! It can make the world a better place because after you see what is going to happen, if it is bad, you can change it. Like if people are going to cut down trees, we will know before they do.

The Futureless is made out of plastic and in the inside it is made out of steel. But it can still hold all the power. It is black. It is not even an inch long, but you can still see it perfectly. It does not make any sounds so you will not have to listen to any sounds to see if it works or not. It will never break. It is impossible. This is how it works. The power in the Futureless will send its power and it will turn the power into videos of the real future to your mind. It will show you when you are daydreaming. If you don't daydream, it will show it to you when you're asleep. That's just if you want to. It will also show it to you whenever you close your eyes.

I will sell the Futureless to a store that the whole world has like Target. It will cost $60. I will sell it to scientists, people who want to help the world, family, friends and famous people. Only people eight years old and over can buy it and use it. People can stockpile by using the Futureless.

The TCRB
By Jacob L.

My invention is called the TCRB, short for TV Computer Robot bed. It can turn into a TV, computer, robot or bed.

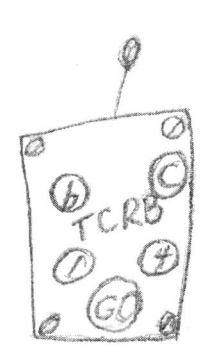

The TCRB is made out of steel. It looks like a small box with a radio signal on it. There are five buttons on the TCRB. One of the buttons has a "t" on it; that stands for TV. There is also "b", "c", "r", and "GO". My invention makes a big beeping sound.

The TCRB is worth $5,000.50. It is for ages five and up. You will be able to find it at Radio Shack, Target, Toys 'R Us and Harris Teeter.

My Incredible Imagination ... Inventions

The Everyday Setter
By Danielle M.

The Everyday Setter is a table setter. The Everyday Setter sets the table for you.

The Everyday Setter looks like Wall-E a little bit. It has a cowboy hat. The Everyday Setter works by solar power. If you say, "Set the table, Table Setter," it sets the table. The Everyday Setter is adjustable for any table. It has hands, arms and wheels for its feet.

My invention will be sold at Target. The Everyday Setter will cost $3.53. I will sell it to my family and friends, too.

The Wonderful Swirl
By Elena H.

My invention is called the Wonderful Swirl because the swirl is its shape. The Wonderful Swirl is easy to work. All you do is ask for whatever you want. **ANYTHING** that you want is OK and in five milliseconds, you have whatever you asked for.

The Wonderful Swirl has a nick-name, the Swirl. The Swirl is mouse-sized, small and rosy red. Here is how it works. A person is hungry. He/She asks for a soda. He/She asks for a cheeseburger. He/She says, "Thank you," and earns $1,000 and 99¢. (**TIP:** Every time you say, "**THANK YOU**" to the Swirl for whatever you asked for, you get $1000 and 99¢!)

The Swirl will be sold at Safeway starting any Monday in November in the year 2050. The sale ends at the last day of November. Mary H. will buy it. Will you?

By Mr. Knott's Bulldogs

3

THE AMAZING BOB
By Emmett K.

My invention is called THE AMAZING BOB. It will put a person in a person's favorite video games and "Voila!," the person is in the machine. The person will be the character that they selected.

THE AMAZING BOB uses solar panels. He is an environmentalist. He is as big as Mr. Knott's class. THE AMAZING BOB works by music.

I will sell THE AMAZING BOB at the video games stores. THE AMAZING BOB will be $1,000. THE AMAZING BOB will be the best seller that I will ever see.

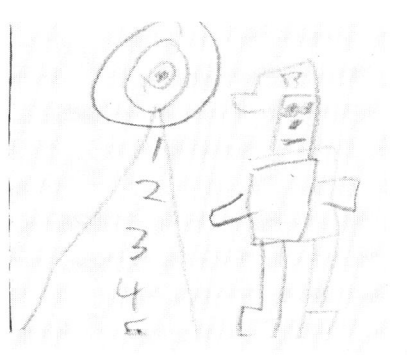

The D.N.A. Machine
By Gabriel M.

The D.N.A Machine can change your D.N.A. You just need to type down your power that you want. For example, super-strength. There are special suits that you are supposed to use if you want to get a power. The suits are made out of scuba diving suits with an astronaut helmet, but all the same color — blue.

The D.N.A. Machine is made out of silver titanium. It looks like a big pod. It has a door that is like an elevator door. And there is a little glass thing that has a switch. You pull the switch up and then some sort of big helmet slowly goes on your head. The suit protects you because it is really tight and it has tentacle things that go on it.

The D.N.A. Machine is going to only cost $1.00 for the military and the police and $1,000 for civilians to use it. It will only be found in police stations. If you want to buy one power, you have to go to a police station or the military.

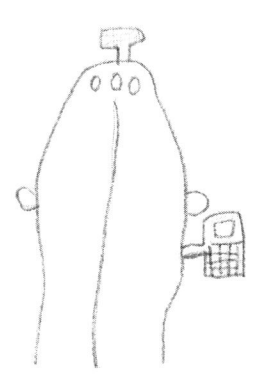

My Incredible Imagination ... Inventions

The Everything
By Sophia C.

My invention is The Everything. It can do everything and if you tell The Everything to do something, it will do it. Like if you say, "Fly me over to the store," it will take you! It also shrinks and unshrinks whatever you want.

The Everything can transform into anything. To make it work, you just say, "Transform." Just say something and you'll get it. The Everything is very helpful.

The Everything will sell at CVS. It will cost about $100. I think people who can't get around that well would want to buy it, but anyone else can still buy it, too.

The Amazing Anything-Bot
By John K.

My invention is called the Amazing Anything-Bot. He is called the Anything-Bot because he does anything you tell him to. If you ask to have $9,999,999.99, he will give you the cash, no questions asked.

The Amazing Anything-Bot has 13 rocket powered jets. The Amazing Anything-BOT is made of titanium, steel and diamond. It comes in all the colors or just ask him to change colors. Here is a suggestion: ask him for an amusement park. If you do, he will make bumper cars, a Ferris wheel, nine roller coasters, an arcade, and anything else he does not make, you have to ask him to make.

I am going to sell the Amazing Anything-Bot globally, which means around the globe. He will be cheap. It will cost $10,000.99. The people who can have one are kids eight to 20 years old. Their parents will have to buy the Amazing Anything-Bot because the kids can't afford it.

By Mr. Knott's Bulldogs 3

The Solar Giant
By Patrick C.

My invention is called the Solar Giant. It is powered by solar panels. The Solar Giant has a smaller ship that astronauts ride from NASA. It has luxurious elevators that take people up hallways.

The Solar Giant has a waterslide in it. The Solar Giant also has a football field and a baseball field, too. It even has a basketball court, a bowling alley and a golf course with artificial turf. The Solar Giant has a pool right next to the waterslide. The Solar Giant has stores to buy toys, clothes and food. The Solar Giant also has a food court if you want to have food from restaurants. For kids, it has three schools and ten video arcades. It also has a Chuck E. Cheese, a fun park and a mini golf course.

You might be thinking the Solar Giant would cost a lot of money but it only cost $100,000. A ticket cost $89.

My invention will help a lot. That is my invention.

The Robot Horse
By Morgan F.

My invention is called a Robot Horse and, if you need a horse, the Robot Horse will be your horse. It can walk, trot, canter and jump.

The Robot Horse is a color that you ask it for. For example, if you want it to turn black, it will turn black. My invention does not sound like a robot, it sounds like a horse that is alive. The Robot Horse has a wheel, axle and screws that make it strong. It has tons of gears, and it has buttons on the bottom of it. The Robot Horse also has on and off buttons. It can eat if you give it horse food. After it digests the food, it will go to the bathroom.

I am going to sell the Robot Horse at Harris Teeter because the kids will like it. It will cost $20.

My Incredible Imagination ... Inventions

The Xtra Technology Piece
By Ben R.

My invention is called Xtra Technology Piece. Call it XTP. It takes hours and hours of entertainment wherever you go! XTP has many features to impress you. Tough math homework is eliminated from your list. A calculator is one of XTP's six features. You should try the phone. When you're in an emergency or you have something to say, the XTP's phone is for you. Who cares about a luxury movie theater? Who cares if your TV is broke? The XTP has a movie player so you can keep your eyes to the screen anywhere! I know a DS is cool, but the XTP has a DS game player! Music is not a care. If your radio is bad, put your CD in the XTP. But try the ordinary computer, the source of the action. Instead of a computer mouse, you use a pen to click on something. Cool, right?

The XTP's look is unique. Its body is the computer, but there's more! There's a spot to put your DS game under the keyboard, (which is under the computer screen). On the right of the computer's keyboard is the pen case. To the left of the keyboard is the CD player. On top of the computer's keyboard is the computer's screen, of course! On the right of the computer's screen is the phone. On the left of the screen is the calculator. So, the look is unique. The only other thing on the look is it's in the shape of a rectangle. But one thing is the same. Like the normal computer, it has a keyboard, a screen, a volume button, whatever your computer has. Trust me. It works by using the pen to control it. Touch whatever you want and then you got it. So, no plugs!

The XTP will be sold at places like CVS, Target, Wal-Mart, Home Depot and any place with electronics. And hear this! You can take off what you don't want so you can get a special price!
Here are the prices:
Everything: $200.99
Minus 1 thing: $170.99
Minus 2 things: $115.99
Minus 3 things: $102.99

Robot Sarah 5
By Miranda M.

My invention is a robot called Sarah 5. It can turn from normal size into pocket size. Sarah 5 can read my mind to help me. She has arms, legs and things like a human except the head is square.

Sarah 5 is undetectable and it only appears when you snap and clap at the same time. It talks like a normal person. The Sarah 5 does chores, has good behavior, and makes its own money.

I'm not going to sell Sarah 5 because I want her for myself. Sarah 5 is priceless!

By Mr. Knott's Bulldogs   3

The Talk, Shop, and Sit
by Claire S.

My invention is called the Talk, Shop, and Sit. It holds the cell phone to the ear. You buy it with $5.00 in the purse. It also has an electronic chair attached to the cell phone structure. The seat has wheels and a steering wheel. It has about two fingers for snapping. It also has free cheeseburgers, soda, orange pops and strawberry shortcake ice cream bars. It has a fold-out McDonald's stand. It also has a fold-out hot pink Lamborghini convertible. If you want soda tops, it gives them to you.

My invention runs on 20 batteries that are not included. It has four wheels. It has an on/off button. It has a seat with pop-out cushions and is perfumed with the smell of roses. It folds up on a chain. It also has a fold-up button and plenty of others. It also has a flashlight.

The Talk, Shop, and Sit is going to cost $100. It will be in stores in the year 2012. It can be used by anyone. It is going to be sold at Target, malls, Costco and Harris Teeter. It is free for anyone in my family. It makes a little 'beep beep' noise.

The Cleaning Android
By Will E.

This is a new invention. It is called The Cleaning Android! The Cleaning Android shoots down dirty stuff. So if you need something cleaned, get one. Don't work hard to clean anything. It cleans the whole house.

The Cleaning Android looks like a robot driving a car. It has four arms. This android has a super-soaking water gun. This water gun has lots of soap and water. The Cleaning Android is five feet tall. It has a sponge, too. It always says "must clean." It is controlled by a remote and transmitter.

The Cleaning Android will be sold at discount stores like Target, Kmart and Walgreens. Anyone can buy it because it only costs a cent.

My Incredible Imagination ... Inventions

My Sports Car
By Miles K.

My invention is called My Sports Car. My Sports Car doesn't need a driver. It can drive where you want. It can carry anything.

My Sports Car can drive 1,000 miles per hour! Lightning can never break through it. It is solar powered. It can turn into a limo, boat, bus or an airplane or a mouse. It can be blue or black. It has wheels. It has an MP3, DVD, CD player, IPod video and a Playstation 3. Six people can fit in it. My Sports Car is fast. It has a key to turn it on. My sports car has a computer ladder to climb in. It has a hole to put the gas in.

I will sell My Sports Car at my house for about $2,000. I think it will sell fast because it is cool. I hope people like my car. I hope I will be famous. I think it is cool!

The Fold-A-House
By Anna R.

My invention is called Fold-a-House. My invention is for people who like to travel. It has a stairway and electricity. It also has a built in vent.

The Fold-a-House is good for camping, because its vents keep you warm instead of a fire. It has double doors, two beds, a stove, two lights, a television, a table and two chairs. When you buy Fold-a-House, the walls are white so you can paint the Fold-a-House if you want. The Fold-a-House does not have a porch.

I will sell the Fold-a-House to a place that sells houses. It will cost $4000. I will sell it to people that like to travel. Forty thousand of these will be made.

By Mr. Knott's Bulldogs

The Rebooting Robot
By Zach R.

My invention is called the Rebooting Robot, or the RR for short. Let me explain what this exciting machine does! Okay, so an iPod needs to be charged, so listen to this. Say you forgot and left your iPod on all night. That's where the Rebooting Robot comes in. You turn a lever to make the plug-in charger really small, attach it to your iPod, and in a second or two… you've got a fully charged iPod! But, if you plug it in too long, the iPod and the RR may explode. So the RR gives things energy. It is the evolved form of the charger.

The RR looks like a robot with small hands, two feet, two miniature arms, a mouth, a nose and two eyes (basically a human with tiny arms). It can be four feet tall or four inches tall. How it can change size gets us to buttons, levers, gears, springs and all about how the RR works. The RR works as a big solar-powered charging machine. Not a battery, not a charger, it replaces both. You could call it the Batplug, too, if you wanted to. It helps saves energy, too. Its outsides are made of steel. The steel is also the first part of the three levels of the body. The second and smallest layer is the Spring Layer. That layer controls the size talked about earlier. The next layer is the Electricity/Energy Layer. It's the power the RR uses to charge. There are three head layers, too. The first is the Water Layer. It's used if you have to shutdown the RR. The second layer is Explosion Layer. That would completely destroy the RR in 15 seconds. The only time you may need to do that is if there is overload. An overload happens when you are loading too much energy into an electronic device. (The result is both ends, the RR and the iPod, explode.) This is why kids under 11 have to be watched. Kids under five can't use it at all. The third layer of the head is the Speech Level. The RR only says "Loading," " OVERLOAD!!!", "Shutdown," and "The RR is currently on."

I would sell the RR to anyone that "cares" for electronic devices and hates storms. It would cost $100.50. I will sell it to all stores that have an electronics section like Target, Wal-Mart and Best Buy.

My Incredible Imagination ... Inventions

The Upperclean
By Rebecca H.

My invention is called Upperclean. The Upperclean will amazingly clean up all of the toys in my whole house!

My Upperclean is an awesome type of robot. But you don't have to control it! It's just like a human. The invention is almost invisible because it's glass and you can sort of see it because of the flashing lights.

I will sell it at almost every store! It will cost $96.15. I think people five years and up will enjoy having this friend around!

The Transformer 5000
By Alex B.

My invention is called the Transformer 5000! It can transform into anything you want!

The Transformer 5000 is made out of red and blue metal and it has 3,009,989 red buttons. It runs by natural gas and it is 20 feet long and six feet wide. The transformer has a Viper engine that can go up to 90,099,867 M.P.H. and has really soft seats! The 3,009,989 buttons will transform into any picture on the button.

My invention will be... ABSOLUTLY FREE!!!!! Only kids will buy it because it is parent-proof!!!! It will be sold at Wal-Mart, CVS, 7-Eleven and at Target.

By Ms. Schaefer's Scholars

3

The Amazing Homework Machine
By Sophie B.

My invention is called the Amazing Homework Machine. It does all homework! The good thing is it saves trees because it makes its own paper. To get the paper, call me. For it to work you need sunlight (but you can use a light bulb). For it to work, you press a button and it quickly starts.

My Amazing Homework Machine is fat like my room and smart like a scholar. It is cool, so everyone who has $2000 will want to buy it.

The Amazing Homework Machine will cost $2000. You can get it at Harris Teeter, my yard, or you can call me to get it! You must be 20 years or older to order.

ORDER NOW!

The Flinch
By Julia F.

The Flinch is a machine that takes you places and even closes the car door! Plus, it also collects the trash. If you get hot while you are traveling, the Flinch comes with drinks.

The Flinch comes with two kinds of lemonade, pink and regular. The lemonade never runs out. In order to travel, there is a chair that is green and sparkly and has stars on it. You press the purple button to start it. The Flinch looks like a palm tree attached to a chair with a table and it has a green glow-in-the-dark hot tub just in case the traveler gets cold.

I will sell The Flinch at the beach. People that travel will want to buy it and probably anyone else.

My Incredible Imagination ... Inventions

The Ultimate Homework Doing Machine 5000
By Ryan B.

My invention is called The Ultimate Homework Doing Machine 5000! It is beneficial, rapid, fantastic and colossal. It is a simple machine and, by the name, you can probably tell that it does any kind of homework, even college homework!

The Ultimate Homework Doing Machine 5000 looks like a big gray metal box with two arms on the side. To use The Ultimate Homework Doing Machine 5000, you just slide the homework in the slot and in a couple of seconds it's done! The Ultimate Homework Doing Machine 5000 can also do any projects, but it takes a little longer to do those.

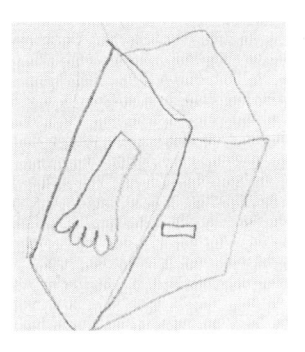

I am probably going to sell The Ultimate Homework Doing Machine 5000 at Circuit City, Target, Best Buy and Wal-Mart. I think everyone will buy it and I am going to sell it for $99.99.

The Super Amazing Flying Backpack
By Nicholas G.

My invention is called the Super Amazing Flying Backpack. It will fly you to school.

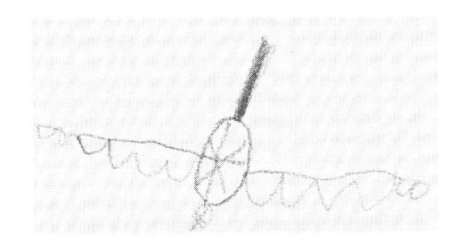

The Super Amazing Flying Backpack is made of plastic, metal, and rubber. Plastic attaches to everything and it runs on AAA batteries! You need to put it on top of a roof for it to work. It attaches to your back with a seatbelt made of thread.

Just press the shiny red button and you will fly. It will cost 80 dollars. I will sell my invention at Toys 'R Us. Eight-year-old kids will want to purchase it if they want to soar. Batteries are not included.

By Ms. Schaefer's Scholars

3

The Everlasting Homework 999,990
By Matt H.

My super invention is called the Everlasting Homework 999,990. It solves all homework from preschool to law school.

The Everlasting Homework 999,990 is a huge, voice-activated supercomputer that processes ten times faster than the brain. It also has a printer. To activate it, you say your grade, for instance "Third," and then you say your subject, "Adaptation," and it prints homework that's never wrong! It has dyed glass that changes to gold and silver in sunlight.

My invention will cost $9,999 and rich people from all over the world will buy it. I will sell it at a market and travel all over the world so everybody can buy it!!

The Rainy Day
By Stephanie S.

One day, it was going to rain, but it did not. The weatherman made a mistake. "Tomorrow it's going to rain a lot," said the weatherman.
I did not worry because I had nothing to do. My dad said, "Let's go to Tia Anna's house." But I said to him, "It's raining". He wanted to have dinner at her house. Instead, my mom cooked food for the family. We had macaroni for dinner. It was very good. I wanted more and more!
After dinner, it stopped raining so I got to go outside. I was playing soccer with my friend. When I was going to kick the ball, I got hurt. Then I went inside. After that, my friend went to her house and asked her mom if she could sleep over at my house. Her mom said she could sleep over.
Then it started to rain again!

Note: Stephanie's story has a different topic because she joined Nottingham after the third graders finished their Invention stories.

My Incredible Imagination ... Inventions

The Amazing Burt
By Emma D.

My invention is an amazing robot! His name is the Amazing Burt. If you want to get him, he can shop, drive, and fly 50 miles per hour!

Burt is a boy and he has red hair (it's really a wig). Burt is really cool! For example, if you wanted a really cool shirt, he could get it! All you have to do is say what to get and where to get it! He's charged by batteries, so you will have to put new batteries in every once and a while. All you have to do is flip up a patch on his back and put the new batteries in.

If you want to buy him, he costs $1000! You will be able to get him at Wal-Mart, no matter what! I'd say if you keep a lot of money in your wallet, you should buy him!

Cool With a K
By Conor C.

My invention is a robot called Cool With a K. My robot can transform into a hot tub or a bed and do your homework.

The homework machine is on the left and the hot tub on the right. The bed is in the middle. Amazingly, the Cool With a K can accommodate 1,000,000 teddy bears on its mattress and it leaves lots of room for you. It runs on solar power.

I will sell Cool With a K at Lowes, Home Depot, and Best Buy. Everyone would buy it. I will sell it for $1000.

By Ms. Schaefer's Scholars

3

Humongous Humanoid
By Adam D.

My new invention is called Humongous Humanoid. Humongous Humanoid will solve the problem of being hot, dry, tired, and bored at the same time! Also it saves lots of time!

Humongous Humanoid is made of rust-proof metal, bronze, glass, plastic, paper, chrome and golden plaster! I named it Humongous Humanoid because it is humongous! My new invention uses a puny generator that can generate 1,000,000,000,000,000,000 volts at a time!

My new invention will cost $2,215. The Humongous Humanoid will be sold at Target, Best Buy, and Circuit City. All ages can buy it if they have the money. Families from higher social classes will buy it because they have the money.

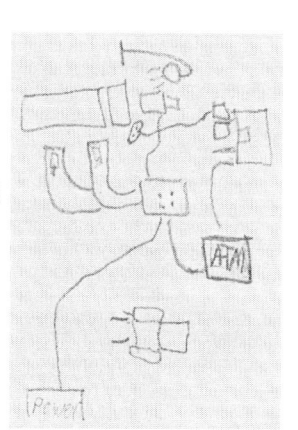

The Teleflage
By Megan T.

My invention is called The Teleflage. It can teleport or even camouflage you.

The Teleflage is as big as a walk-in closet. On each side there are panels. On one panel there is a switch that you can push to teleport or camouflage. On the other panel there is a small hand scanner. To make the Teleflage work, you must scan your hand on the small hand scanner. When it starts, it has light bulbs that glow and get brighter then brighter, then ZAP! If you wanted to camouflage yourself, you would walk out and be camouflaged. If you wanted to be teleported, before the lights start flashing there is a small screen that looks like a keyboard and you type in where you want to go. Then hit the "go" button and off you go!

The Teleflage will cost $9,999.90. It will be sold at Wal-mart. Only extremely rich people would buy it and my friends and family because they get a $9,999 discount.

My Incredible Imagination ... Inventions

Amazing Robot
By Shelby B.

My invention is called the Amazing Robot. It can do anything and make everything.

My invention looks 500 feet tall, but it is really 200 feet tall. It can also read people's minds. My robot has 100 buttons. If you press one, for instance, it might give you a jumbo pizza. My invention will cost $50 to $100. I think Mary, Megan H. and Megan T. or other people will buy it.

You guys can buy it at Wal-Mart or Target. Does anyone want to buy my lovely Amazing Robot?

Homework Doing Machine
By Ryan M.

My invention is called the Homework Doing Machine. It will do your homework even if you're an adult or a kid.

The assignment needs to be on paper. The Homework Doing Machine is made of metal. You may choose a color: yellow, gray, blue, green, white, purple, or silver. When you press ON, it will turn on the brain and when you press OFF, it will turn off the brain. Then you put your homework in the machine. Then the scanner will scan the homework and send the information to the brain. Then the brain will activate the hand holding the pen. Next, the hand holding the pen will write the answers.

The Homework Doing Machine will cost $1,000. I will sell it at computer stores. Kids and adults will want to buy it. The Homework Doing Machine must plug into the wall to power the machine.

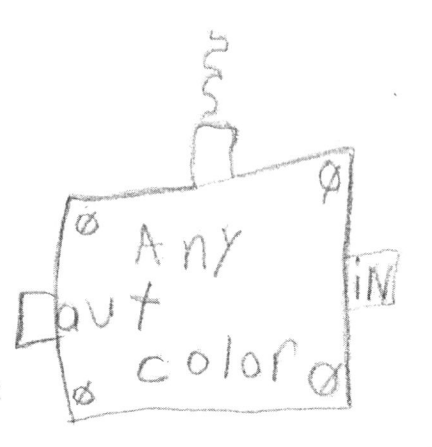

By Ms. Schaefer's Scholars

3

Awesome Book Maker
By Allie S.

My cool invention is called Awesome Book Maker. My cool invention helps people write amazing books.

The Awesome Book Maker looks like shiny, smooth metal. It's square-shaped and the size of a refrigerator. It simply works by putting a piece of paper in it, pressing a button and saying, "Funny", if you want a funny story, and the book comes out.

My awesome invention will only cost $20. The awesome invention will be sold at the end of my street. I think everybody will buy it because it is cool!

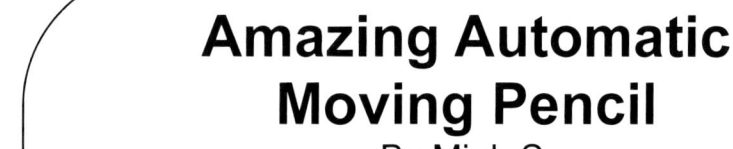

Amazing Automatic Moving Pencil
By Minh S.

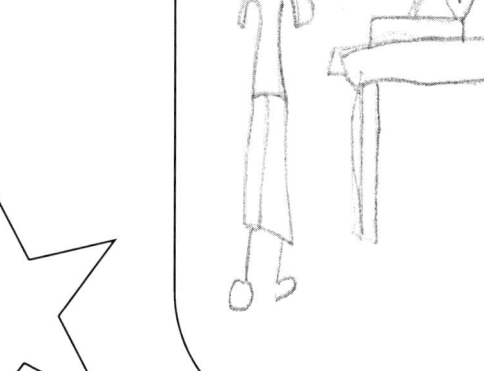

My creative invention is called the Amazing Automatic Moving Pencil. It writes automatically when you speak.

My Amazing Automatic Moving Pencil is made of eraser and has a microphone. It can be designed in any color and it is held up by energy in the air. It has to use AAA batteries, but they do not come with it.

The Amazing Automatic Moving Pencil will cost two to four dollars. I will sell it at Target. Anyone can buy it: Mom, Dad, sister or brother.

My Incredible Imagination ... Inventions

Tonnert Gold Mach 9 Jet Pack
By Sean K.

My invention is the Tonnert Gold Mach 9 Jet Pack. It will let Navy dudes go places in a snap.

My invention looks like a gray box (you can simply paint it for upgraded ranks). Coming out of the gray box on the top is a missile. On the sides are two circles with rectangles coming off the bottom. Two triangles with their tops cut off serve as the thrusters. It goes fast because 17 electro-shock fuel energizers make it move more quickly. The missile on top has 7 electro-shockers and two long-range AS-51 fuel cartridges with two electro-shock fuel energizers.

My invention will cost $356. Navy dudes can purchase it at a Navy warehouse in 2x4 boxes. Navy dudes would want to buy it for top secret missions.

Awesome Tron 5,000,000
By James M.

My Invention is called the Awesome Tron 5,000,000. It can take away gravity and make good food like pizza and pie. My invention can print real money (my copy only) then buy me stuff like toys and video games. My invention can do homework (in your handwriting by first scanning your hand). It can make really cool jet packs like those you would see on TV.

It looks like an average toy robot! My invention is five feet tall and two feet across. There is a slot to put homework (pre-school to law school) and a slot in the back to take your homework out of! It's amazing!!! My invention zaps you in a bubble that can't be popped, then you can walk in mid-air!

It would cost one million dollars. I would make it myself. I would sell it at Wal-Mart, Target, and Radio Shack!

By Ms. Schaefer's Scholars

The Automatic Opening Door
By Linh S.

My invention is called the Automatic Opening Door! It will make it more exciting and easier for you to open the door. It is like a regular door, but it is not the same. You have the door and keyhole but you leave the keys at home. Then the excitement starts! See, it goes like this.

When you get up to go to school or work, you will put the keys in a little elevator and the elevator automatically stops the keys so when you come home, the keys will be waiting. Then you will say, "May I have my keys?" When they come, you put them in the keyhole then the door goes up! Amazing! Then you walk underneath it and it closes. It also has a sensor so when you walk underneath the door, it will tell if you are the right person. If not, an alarm will go off! The next door neighbors will come and call the police.

The Automatic Opening Door will cost $900-$1,000. The price depends on the shape, style, and color. I will sell it at Home Depot. I think a rich person or a grown-up will buy it. My Invention runs by air.

My Incredible Imagination ... Inventions

The $.$. Spender
By Katherine B.

The $.$. Spender is a robot that will take you shopping in New York, Paris, L.A. and Japan. It can take you on movie sets like Harry Potter and has a built in iPod and Wii. It pretty much buys anything you want and has doughnut feet.

The $.$. Spender makes noise from the Wii games and when it buys something, there is a big "chuh ching!" My invention runs on soda bottles. If you don't have any soda bottles, you can also buy a charger for $30.00.

The $.$. Spender will be about $500.00. It will be sold at Party City, Best Buy, and Target. So…GO BUY IT!

The Massaginator 2000
By Matthew N.

My invention is called the Massaginator 2000. The Massaginator 2000 massages sore feet.

My invention looks like a box with four hands - two hands to walk on and two hands to massage your feet. The Massaginator 2000 does not make any noise. It moves soundlessly everywhere it goes. The Massaginator 2000 works on two AA batteries. All you have to do is press the letter button of your first name and the Massaginator 2000 massages you.

I will sell my invention at Circuit City and wherever electronics are sold. It would cost $999.99 because it is very comfortable. I think track and field people would buy it because they get sore feet a lot. I also think athletes would buy it because they get sore feet a lot, too!
That is my invention.

By Mrs. Stewart's Superstars

Solar Chips
By Jake B.

My invention is Solar Chips. Solar Chips have a special type of solar panel attached on them. The solar panel is activated by air. So please don't attach them to your car and then drive to a place without air!

Solar Chips look like a stop watch with a lever, a small screen, and six buttons. There is a small solar panel and two antennas. On the bottom, there's the best type of Gorilla Glue that can only be removed by a special tool to hold on the solar panel. You can also play music by using the software chip that comes with Solar Chip packets that works on PC, Mac, Windows, Dell, and Apple ONLY!! Download songs onto this chip, plug it into any Solar Chip, and play music! It's voice activated, so whenever you want to listen to your music just say, "Solar Chip, play me something."

You will be able to find Solar Chips at hardware stores, Target, Macys, Wal-Mart, and Starbucks, even at hotels! Actually, Solar Chips can be found anywhere you can buy or rent anything. They only cost $1.99 and never break! Solar Chips can do your homework. Anyone will be able to enjoy Solar Chips and NO global warming! So, go out there and buy Solar Chips TODAY!!!!!!!!!!!!

The Phone Pod
By Will A.

My name for my invention is the Phone Pod. It is kind of like an iPhone but more advanced.

The Phone Pod is a little bigger than a ball and it runs on a battery. It is like a phone but with more things.

I will sell the Phone Pod at Target. It costs $700.00.

My Incredible Imagination ... Inventions

The Amazing Everything Bed
By Audrey V.

The Amazing Everything Bed can do anything, even your homework.

Just put your homework in the Amazing Everything Bed and in moments your homework is done! It's really amazing. The Amazing Everything Bed can turn into anything. It can give you anything, too. If your house is messy and needs cleaning, press "Clean Now" and in moments it will be clean. The Everything Bed is very useful. It's portable. Just press "Pocket Size."

The Everything Bed costs $1.00 at every store. You should buy it. It's wonderful.

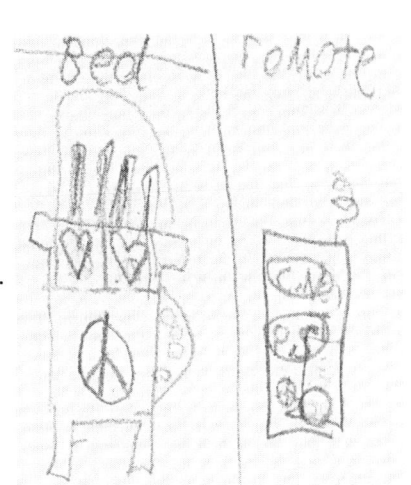

The Soldier Setter
By Ben B.

The name of my invention is the Soldier Setter. It sets up your toy soldiers so you don't need to do it.

The Soldier Setter sees by a camera. It's on a timer so you have to know the minutes. It looks like a Wall-e. The Soldier Setter makes no sounds. The Soldier Setter sets only one pack of troops.

I think that more boys than girls will buy the Soldier Setter. I will sell it at Wal-Mart for only $5.99. People can buy one and get one for free.

By Mrs. Stewart's Superstars

Do-What-A-Ma-Call-It
By Jennifer L.

My invention is called Do-What-A-Ma-Call-It. It does anything you want a Do-What-A-Ma-Call-It to do.

The Do-What-A-Ma-Call-It is green, blue and red. When you press the #1 button on the machine and say, "Do Homework," the Do-What-A-Ma-Call-It will do your homework. The Do-What-A-Ma-Call-It does not make any sound. The machine is made from metal. To make the machine work, you put a water bottle filled with orange juice in it, wait 30 seconds, and it will power up.

I will sell the Do-What-A-Ma-Call-It on Ebay. The machine will cost $1500.99. Everybody will want to buy it.

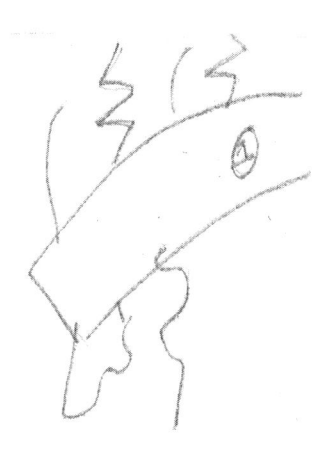

The Amazing Everything Seat
By Sophia G.

My invention is called the Amazing Everything Seat. It makes noises like beep, bloop, and bop when you press a button.

When you press the green button on the Amazing Everything Seat, a TV comes up. Here are some of the things that it can do. It can turn into a bed. If you clap twice, a TV pops up. If you pull the red lever, there is an amazing back massager. If you press the blue button, you get a foot massage and if you press the pink button and say a type of food, that particular food pops up! It can get lots of other stuff like that too. My invention looks like a big huge chair with a blanket and 100 pillows, for when it turns into a bed. It also has a built in Slurpee/Coca-Cola machine!

I will sell the Amazing Everything Seat for about $800.00. So... GO BUY IT!!!!!!!!!!

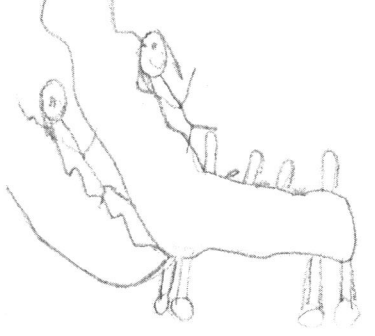

My Incredible Imagination ... Inventions

Cooling and Heating Boots
By Jason L.

My invention is called Cooling and Heating Boots. They cool and heat feet.

The Cooling and Heating Boots look like regular boots. Amazingly, they know when your feet are hot or cold. They have vents and a button to turn them on.

You will be able to buy Cooling and Heating Boots at a shoe store. They will be sold for 21 cents.

The Present Wrapper
By Sam M.

My invention is called the Present Wrapper. It lets you wrap presents and design wrapping paper. It is somewhat easy to use.

To use the Present Wrapper, you push the green button and then it pings. After that, the Present Wrapper asks you if you'd like to wrap or design. If you choose wrap, you insert your present then it wraps it for you. If you choose design, some symbols appear on the touch pad like a menorah or Santa.

The Present Wrapper will be sold at Target for $50. People who give a lot of presents will buy it.

By Mrs. Stewart's Superstars

The Room Cleaner
By Natasha L.

My invention is called a Room Cleaner. It can clean one room in a minute. It can also vacuum everything it can see.

The Room Cleaner looks weird but it is helpful. It's made out of metal. It has buttons, cleaners, wipers, two vacuum cleaners, eyes, a shelf cleaner, clothes picker-uppers, and special sticky stuff to climb walls. My invention has special buttons that have numbers on them. Button# 1 is the button that makes the invention walk on walls and clean the walls. Button # 2 makes the invention clean clothes and rugs. Button #3 makes the invention pick up clothes. There is also one special button that makes the invention do everything at the same time! That button can do all the work while you are doing something else, like walking your dog.

My invention is going to be sold in Safeway. It would cost $2.99. I think parents would mostly like to buy it.

The Secret Cave
By Miles M.

My invention is a secret cave. It is fun to play in.

The Secret Cave has all the things I need. It is in my backyard underground. I play in it when my mom says I can't play video games. It could help you do your homework and tell you all the answers. It comes with vibrating chairs.

The Secret Cave is sold at Home Depot. If you want to buy it, come and buy it today!!!!!!!!!!!!!!!!!!

My Incredible Imagination ... Inventions

The Food Box
By Julia D.

The name of my invention is Food Box. If you're tired of buying so much food for so much money, then this will solve your problem.

The Food Box is a small little box that can fit in your pocket. It can come in many different shapes and colors! This invention runs on energy, so if it doesn't work just shake it up and it's back on track! It's made of extremely hard metal so it will be hard to break. The food never gets stale! There are lots of buttons so you can pick which food you like. There's a little tiny guard that guards your food! P.S. Your guard makes sure you can't sell your food.

The Food Box will be sold in the Super Store next to the Four Sider. It costs a thousand dollars. This is pretty much for grown-ups because with kids, it could get out of control. Well, I hope you like it!!!! So..........GO BUY IT!!!!!!!!!!!!!

The Quick Cleaner
By Kirsten K.

My invention is a robot that can clean up your room and dust! It's called the Quick Cleaner.

At night time, you can press a button on the Quick Cleaner and it will shrink down to the size of a lunch box! You can store it anywhere! If you spill something, just call the Quick Cleaner and it will clean it up! It can tell time and be an alarm clock! If you get lonely you can talk to it! My invention can get taller and shorter to reach high and low. Its arms can also grow.

The Quick Cleaner will be sold for $25.95. It will be sold at Target, Wal-Mart, and Staples. The Quick Cleaner takes batteries. It has four buttons. If you're a mom or a dad and you're tired of cleaning, you should buy the Quick Cleaner!

By Mrs. Stewart's Superstars

The Video Game Killer
By Nick B.

My invention is called The Video Game Killer. It is good for when you are frustrated at a video game and you really can't beat a level.

The Video Game Killer is metal, aluminum, and it is not hollow. The Video Game Killer has balls where limbs bend just like us. My invention only takes Duracell batteries and they have to be 9 volt, too. The Video Game Killer takes seven batteries at a time. The Video Game Killer is almost four feet tall and about one foot wide. The Video Game Killer has wheels on its feet. You don't have to set up the video game for The Video Game Killer — it sets it up for you.

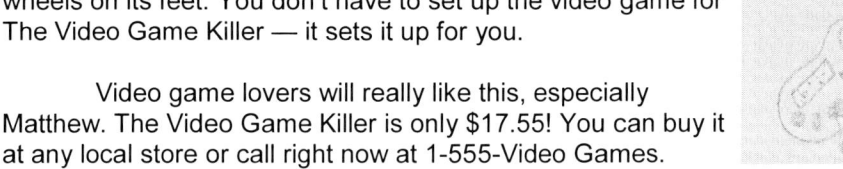

Video game lovers will really like this, especially Matthew. The Video Game Killer is only $17.55! You can buy it at any local store or call right now at 1-555-Video Games.

The Four Sider
By Maya N.

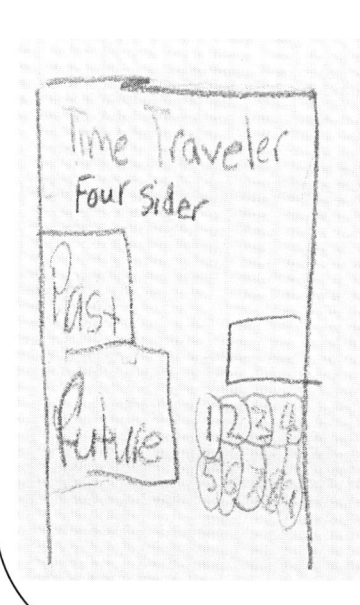

My invention is the Four Sider. It is a box that has four amazing things on each side of it.

If you have ever wanted four amazing things in one box, this is the box for you. On the first side is the time traveler. Here you can type in what time you want to go to whether it is five minutes or 100 years in the future or past. On the next side is the room decorator which decorates any room by just pushing a button. Then the next side is the store zoom where you can go to Safeway, CVS or Target. Finally, there is the super power side where you can choose three super powers of your choice. (Please note that there is already a shrink remote.) The Four Sider runs on one AA battery at a time.

You can buy the Four Sider at the super store next to the Food Box. The Four Sider costs $600.00 and anyone can buy it! So come and buy the Four Sider today!

My Incredible Imagination ... Inventions

No Name Pill
By Michael R.

My Invention is a pill. It doesn't have a name. The pill brushes your teeth for you. One pill=two days.

The pill is small. It doesn't make a sound. The pill softens in your mouth.

You can buy my pill at Wal-Mart and Safeway. It costs $3.99. Everyone will buy it.

The Flying Fan
By Luke S.

My invention is the Flying Fan.

The flying fan is small. It runs on water. It boils the water and then it uses the steam for the spark plug. It is very quiet.

I am going to sell the Flying Fan for $651.99. You can buy it at Radio Shack. I think people that don't like walking in front of fans would buy it. So rev up your cars and come to Radio Shack today!!!

By Mrs. Stewart's Superstars

The Flower Detector
By Alex B.

My invention is the Flower Detector. It helps people find a kind of flower.

The Flower Detector looks like a calculator and makes a beeping sound. The Flower Detector takes pictures of flowers and tells you what kind of flower they are. My invention doesn't really make many sounds. It only makes a beeping sound.

I will sell the Flower Detector for $50.00. I will sell it on the Internet. I think mostly girls are going to buy it.

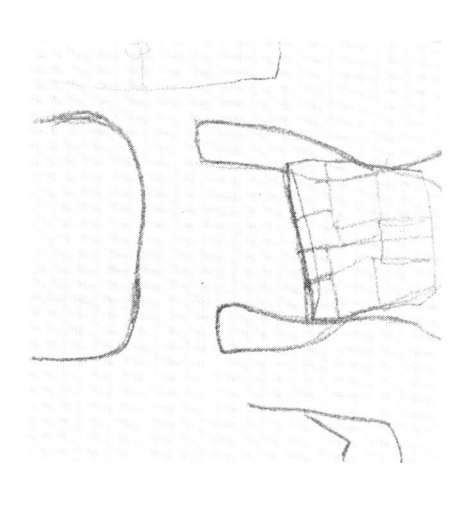

Let's Discover ... Our World

Exploring India
By Matthew F.

If you like eating spicy food, seeing outstanding views, are interested in different cultures and are an elephant lover…go to India!

India is the seventh biggest country in the world. It has the biggest democracy in the world. India has a coastline of 7,517 kilometers, which is a little more then 4,670 miles. Did you know that India has more then 1,000,000,000 people? The capital of India is New Delhi. Did you know that the president of India is Pratibha Patil?

If you go to India, you will meet different people. India has an interesting religion. Their religion is called Hindu. Hinduism is also referred to Sanātana Dharma, which means eternal law. You cannot understand much of India without understanding their religion. The Hindu religion has 330 million gods but their supreme god (main god) is Brahma.

The people of India are very famous for making spices. Another part of their culture is dancing and music. India has more farmland then you can imagine. Some of the crops they grow are rice, corn and peppers.

India is a country to visit and explore. When you have some extra money and you want to visit an interesting place in the world, go to INDIA!

Almost Dead in North Korea
By Michael S.

Imagine being in North Korea, trapped, barely alive on the edge of survival not knowing what is happening in any other place in the world!!!!

Well, that's what thousands of people have experienced for their entire lives! North Korea is a communist country that has been around for many, many years. Communism is their form of government. In a Communist nation, leaders rule people against their own will. This is happening in North Korea right now. Kim Jong II is their communist leader.

Recently, one person dreamed of a better life than he had, so he tried to escape North Korea! He and his friend tried to escape but sadly, his friend died trying to jump over an electric fence. The other man used his friend's body to climb the electric fence to South Korea!! He was the first person known to escape from North Korea! It is believed that approximately 30,000 people have escaped from North Korea over the years but actual totals are unknown.

Perhaps this man's escape is a giant step for mankind and will encourage others in their attempts to escape the strong rule of this communist land.

Fourth grade students used online resources including **timeforkids.com**, **loc.gov**, **nationalgeographic.com**, and **culturegrams.com** along with personal experience as sources of information for their feature/news articles.

By Ms. Barber's Barbershop 4

San Francisco
By Zachary K.

An island that was once used as a prison, an earthquake that caused 700 deaths, and a bridge that is called the Golden Gate Bridge ... these are all cool things you can see in San Francisco!

San Francisco is a city located in the state of California on the western coast of the United States. San Francisco is located on a fairly big bay.

Alcatraz Island is a famous island in the San Francisco bay. Alcatraz Island is also called "The Rock." It is famous because it used to be a jailhouse. The island was also used as a military fortification and a lighthouse until 1963. Although it is not in use now as any of these things, it is still open to tourists for all to see.

San Francisco is also known all over the world for its Golden Gate Bridge. The Golden Gate Bridge was the largest suspension bridge when it was built in 1937. Did you know that 528,000,000,000 gallons of water run under the Golden Gate Bridge every six hours? It is also one of the most popular bridges in the U.S.

An unfortunate thing happened in San Francisco. In 1906, San Francisco had one of its most memorable natural disasters in history. At 5:12 a.m. an earthquake struck that lasted between 45-60 seconds! The shaking was so intense, it was felt from Oregon to Los Angeles, killing 700 people.

San Francisco is known for many great things. There is the Golden Gate Bridge, China Town, and many other great tourist destinations. Plan your trip today!!!

Chicago, IL
By Adam S.

Have you ever been to Chicago? It's a place where buildings are so high, you can't see the top. There's food you can't stop eating, a train five times your size located above ground, and close to 3,000,000 people! It is home of Chicago's World Fair. It is so big, you can't see one side of the city from the other and you could barely walk there in a day. So much to see, no time to do it, but read some more and then you can!

Chicago is located in the middle of North America, in the state of Illinois. It sits on the edge of Lake Michigan.

Chicago is famous for food, especially hot dogs. Their hot dogs are so good that when I visit, our family's first meal is from Portillos, a hot dog restaurant. Their steak is also fabulous! There's even such a thing as the Chicago Grill. If you visit, eat plenty of food.

Another important attraction in Chicago is the Sears Tower. The Sears Tower is famous because of its height. It is 1,457 feet tall. The Sears Tower is one of the tallest buildings in the world. The Water Tower isn't as tall but it's famous because it survived the Chicago fire which burned almost half the city and it still stands today!

Be sure to visit Chicago for great food, exciting attractions, and much, much, more!

Let's Discover ... Our World

St. John
By Claire B.

The water is so clear that you can see the minnows and pebbles beneath your feet. You can walk to ruins and climb a lighthouse. These are just a few of the amazing experiences you will have if you visit the Caribbean.

One of the many Caribbean islands is St. John. St. John is one of the few islands in the Caribbean that does not have an airport. To get to the other islands, you have to take a ferry boat.

St. John is a medium-sized island. On one side, there are rolling mountains that sink into a rocky beach. On the other side, there are lots of trees and vines and a big white beach.

St. John is a great place to go snorkeling. St. John has many snorkeling chains. When you go snorkeling, you can experience the beautiful fish and coral reefs up close.

St. John has many varieties of sea creatures. There's one sea anemone that has black thorns and is shaped in a ball. The most popular fish in the Caribbean is the angel fish. There are many different types of angel fish that live on the reefs in St. John.

If you enjoy all these things, St. John is the place for you!

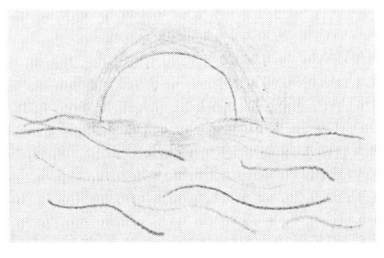

China
By Amelia J.

Have you ever wanted to go to a spectacular, ancient place where they eat rice, wheat, potatoes, and drink tea? If yes, then visit China.

China is located in Asia. It is a very large country. It is only slightly smaller than the United States.

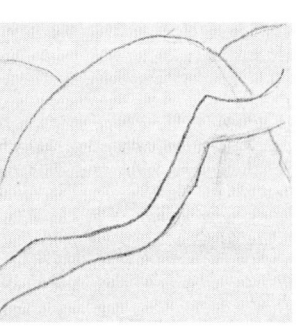

If you visited China, you would have a variety of activities to do. One the most popular things is visit The Great Wall of China. It is the only man-made object you can see from space. Men started making this 4,000 mile long wall 170 years B.C. (before Christ)!

Another interesting historic sight is the carving of the Grand Buddha. The Grand Buddha was carved on the face of a cliff. It is a 233 foot long carving. His ears are 23 feet long! His eyebrows are 13 feet long. It took 95 years to build the Grand Buddha.

Did you know that the Chinese invented a lot of the things that we use today? Well, it's true. Chinese invented fireworks, paper, toys, ice-cream, noodles and a lot of other things.

So, if you are interested in any of these things, then China is the place to visit!

By Ms. Barber's Barbershop

Iraqi Journalist Throws Shoes at Former President George W. Bush
By Ellie S.

On Dec. 14, 2008 in Baghdad, Iraq, an Iraqi journalist threw two shoes at former President George W. Bush. Bush did not get hurt. Instead, he dodged the shoes. The Iraqi journalist threw the shoes because hurling shoes at someone or sitting so that the bottom of a shoe faces another person is considered an insult among the muslins.

The thrower of the shoes was named Al-Zaidi. He threw his size 10 shoes at Bush before he was dragged out of the building. While he was dragged away, Al-Zaidi possibly said something in Arabic that was not very nice. After the shoes were thrown, Bush joked around about it and he didn't seem to be too upset that Al-Zaidi threw the shoes at him.

During the last twenty years, there has been a conflict between Iraq and the United States. The United States has had a foreign policy toward Iraq since the 1930's. A foreign policy is a plan that a country has on how to deal with other countries. In the early 1980's, the Reagan administration actively sought friendly relations with Iraq with great success. Unfortunately, these good relations have been broken down during the last couple of years.

Hopefully President Obama will make peace with the Iraqis during his administration!

Costa Rica
By David B.

If you wanted to visit a place where you can go rafting in the Pacuare River and zipping through the Monteverde Cloud Forest, go to Costa Rica! Costa Rica has nice hotels and beaches. You can learn some Spanish and French because that's their language. In addition, they also speak some English.

Costa Rica is located on the Caribbean Sea in Central America. It is about the size of New Hampshire and Vermont combined. It is also twice the size of Israel. It takes about 3-4 hours by airplane to go from Virginia to Costa Rica.

The religion in Costa Rica is mainly Catholic (76 percent). The national bird is Yoguirro (clay-colored robin). The national flower is Cattleya Skinneri. It is one of the most common orchids in Costa Rica. The national tree is the Guanacaste tree. It was declared the national tree on Aug. 31, 1959.

There are many volcanoes in Costa Rica. You can go and look at the volcano from the top!! When you are in an airplane, you can see the volcanoes. There are a couple you can look at.

So, come look at all these wonderful places in Costa Rica and have fun!

Let's Discover ... Our World

The Facts About Iran
By Bennett C.

Have you wondered what it would be like to live in Iran, to go to school and play in Iran? If you have, then this article is for you!

Iran (pronounced ee-ron) is a country located in the Middle East. It is an Islamic state. It is very different from our country. In Iran, 98 percent of the population is Muslim. The government is totally Islamic. Islam is a religion that follows the teachings of the prophet Muhammad. They believe that he was sent by Allah (God). So if you live in Iran, your religion is probably Islam.

After the revolution in Iran, the government took total control of education. They purged textbooks, teachers, and courses that were "non-Islamic." Even behavior and dress had to be Islamic!!!

The country of Iran is run by an Islamic government. The ultimate decision-maker and the religious head of the government is the faqih. An elected president is responsible for selecting a prime minister and a cabinet. Opposition parties exist in exile abroad (out of the country). Opposition parties are opposed to the government. Some of the opposition parties are monarchists, democrats, Kurds, Islamic groups and Marxists.

So, if you want to visit a place very different from the United States of American, go to Iran!

Chile
By Andrew K.

Have you ever wanted to travel long distances to South America? Have you ever wanted to venture through dark, scary rainforests? Do you want to climb to the top of the third tallest mountain in the world that's covered in snow? Do you want to see leatherback sea turtles that live for over 100 years race to the Galapagos Islands? Have you ever wanted to taste foods that you've never even heard of before? Then Chile is the place for you.

Chile is in South America. It borders Argentina to the east, Peru to the north and Bolivia to the northeast. Chile is a country with amazing foods and great places to visit! You can visit Easter Island. Easter Island contains many rocks with faces in them that ancient people created. These rocks are called the Moai Statues of Rapa Nui (Easter Island). There are only 110 people that live on Easter Island so it is a great place to visit!

In February, giant leatherback sea turtles are going on a 750-mile race from Costa Rica to the Galapagos Islands. Some turtles will swim even further down south to the chilled, icy waters of Chile. This "race" (actually a migration) is supposed to educate people on how important it is to save sea turtles.

Chile is a very exciting place with incredible places to visit so whenever you have free time, visit Chile!

By Ms. Barber's Barbershop   4

Australia
By Anna O.

Do you know where the Great Barrier Reef is located? Do you know where Kangaroo Island is located? They are both located in Australia!

Australia is both a continent and a country. It is in the southern half of the world.

The Great Barrier Reef is the largest coral reef in the world and the only living thing on Earth that can be seen from space. The Great Barrier Reef is 1,250 miles long. There are 400 kinds of coral in the reef. It has lots of animals, including dolphins and birds. The Great Barrier Reef is their home.

The third largest island that is part of Australia is Kangaroo Island. It is home to some of the most well-preserved wildlife in the world. It is only 90 miles long and 34 miles wide. Kangaroos live there and so do koalas, kookaburras, snakes, spiders and fleas.

Tasmania is part of Australia but it is also an island. Tasmanian wilderness is home to wallabies, penguins, black cockatoos, white-bellied sea eagles, seals, dolphins and whales.

Doesn't Australia sound like a amazing place to visit?

Tasmanian Trouble
By Carly C.

One day, you are walking along in Tasmania, an island in the Pacific Ocean south of Australia, when you hear a horrible noise. You turn around and see a cute, brown animal scurry away. You have just seen a Tasmanian devil.

Tasmanian devils were once endangered because farmers killed them, blaming them for the loss of their lambs. As of right now, they are not extinct. When devils are hungry, they eat 40 percent of their body weight. That's like a human eating a 60-pound steak in one sitting!

Although farmers are no longer their worry, they have another problem. A cancer of the lymphatic system is spreading over the population. The lymphatic system defends diseases such as viruses, bacteria and fungi. Scientists are puzzled as to how this came to be. The devil gets very thin even though it eats a tremendous amount of food. In four to six months, the devil dies. Scientists are keeping more Tasmanian devils in captivity. The captive ones don't have the disease. I hope the disease stops spreading and they can let the captive devils go. Only time will tell.

Let's Discover ... Our World

Norway
By Christian C.

Did you ever wonder where Santa gets his reindeer? If you have, well, here is a fact: he gets them from Norway, of course. Norway is a country located in northern Europe. In the summers, it never ever gets dark, so that is why they call it the "land of the midnight sun."

Did you know that Norway is ranked fifth in producers of hydropower in the world? Hydropower is power that comes from water. Norway does not need to buy gas or oil from other countries because they meet all their needs from hydropower.

Did you know that some teens in Norway go to other countries to spend one of their high school years? While there, they study the countries' cultures, history and ways of life.

Most Norwegians enjoy hiking. That's because Norway has so many beautiful mountains. From GaldhØpiggen to SnØhetta, Norway is one of the most fun -filled places to hike or climb

Norway makes most of its money through the harvesting and processing of fish. From lobsters and crabs to salmon and spring cod, Norway catches it all.

Whether you enjoy fishing, learning, hiking, or just having a good time, Norway is the place for you. I hope you enjoyed our visit to Norway. Goodbye.

Australia's Amazing Animals
By Lucille S.

Have you ever seen wallabies? Do you want to? Well, go to Australia and Tasmania. There are tons of them!

Australia is both a continent and a country located halfway around the world in the southern hemisphere. Tasmania is an island located off the coast of Australia. It is about the same size as Scotland.

In Tasmania, there are many unique animals, such as wallabies, penguins, black cockatoos, white-bellied sea eagles, seals, dolphins and whales. Wallabies have a pouch to carry their young in. When the young is too big for the pouch, the mother leaves the young behind while she goes to get water. A baby wallaby drinks from its mother's mouth.

Did you know that the Great Barrier Reef can be seen from space? Well, now you do. The Great Barrier Reef is located off the eastern coast of Australia. It is home to brightly colored fish, 400 types of coral, birds, whales, dolphins and turtles. Most people go snorkeling to see these animals when they visit there. Many marine biologists study the animals that live on the reef.

Australia and Tasmania are amazing places with extraordinary sea life and awesome animals. Most people come to see these animals while some people just come to relax. So, visit Australia and Tasmania today!

By Ms. Barber's Barbershop   4

News From Italy
By Kiara J.

Things are changing in the Trestevere neighborhood of Rome. Giocardo Beso owns a bar there that is more than 70 years old. Many of his old customers do not come to the bar anymore. They are gone. Why?

More and more visitors are buying homes in Trestevere. House prices are rising and many old timers cannot afford to live there. They are moving away. According to Giocardo Beso, when they left they took the spirit of the bar with them. Now he has nobody to talk to. His once special bar is now a regular bar.

Another interesting piece of news from Italy comes from Tuscany. In Tuscany, there is a deer with one antler. This unique animal is drawing the attention of the research center in the Tuscan town of Prato. Scientists think that he was born with a genetic flaw because his brother has two antlers. The researchers nicknamed him "Unicorn."

I think Italy is a great place to visit. I heard they have really good ice cream. I really want to visit Italy.

Giant Pandas
By Lucy K.

The giant panda is one of the largest animals in the world. They live in southwest China. Giant pandas live in trees. When giant pandas have their babies, they live in caves.

The only things giant pandas eat are bamboo, leaves and more bamboo! In the winter it is hard for them to find food. So, they look for food for a very long time.

Surprisingly, giant pandas hate deep water! They only go in shallow water to have a drink. Sometimes, they don't even go in the water!

Giant pandas are relatives of bears. Their colors are different and so are their teeth! Their attitudes are similar, but not by much.

The giant panda is almost extinct. That's why people are starting to bring giant pandas to national zoos around the world. If you see a giant panda in a zoo, it is there for a reason.

Let's Discover ... Our World

Acid Rain In Germany
By Owen M.

Have you ever wondered why forests in Germany are disappearing? Why more and more people are getting asthma? How historic buildings and statues could be in decay? The answer is acid rain. Acid rain can be caused by pollutants that are released into the air.

Acid rain can affect us. One major way is how it affects our lungs. Many people in Germany have asthma because of acid rain. Everything they eat, drink and breathe has once come in contact with an acid deposit. This could make them very sick!

Some forests in Germany are starting to rot and disappear because of acid rain. Acid rain, fog and vapor are killing trees by harming the leaves and needles. In 1983, surveys in western Germany showed that 34 percent of Germany's forests are dying from air pollution, including half of the famous black forest! In the eastern half of Germany, the damage is even worse! This is because factories are making much more air pollution. Germany is the most polluted country in Europe.

Acid rain cannot only harm living things. It can also affect nonliving things, too. It can damage building materials and paints. It can also damage the irreplaceable buildings, statues and sculptures that Germany wants to last a long time. Let's hope that does not happen.

Ghana
By Rachael C.

Would you ever want to go somewhere very different from here? Would you like to visit a tribe that still lives like it has for hundreds of years? Then you should visit Ghana!

Ghana is a country located in Africa. It sits on the Gulf of Guinea. The name Ghana means "warrior king." Ghana has a tropical climate that varies depending on the elevation.

One of the most interesting tribes in Ghana is the Ewe (pronounced ee-wee). The Ewe is one of the main tribes that runs Ghana. The tribe is ruled by a chief. When the chief dies, the son becomes the chief. They speak one language. The Ewe are mainly farmers but they also specialize in crafts such as weaving kente cloth. Kente cloth is special cloth with geometrical designs.

Another important tribe in Ghana is the Ashanti of Akan. This is Ghana's largest tribe. Half of Ghana's population came from this one tribe. They speak a language call *Twi*. In this tribe, uncles are very important and support their sisters' children. They also make kente cloth as well as pottery.

Ghana is a very interesting place where you can see tribes living very differently than you do. I hope you visit there someday.

By Ms. Barber's Barbershop   4

Shoes Being Thrown
By Thomas M.

Have you ever imaged having a shoe thrown at you? Having the sole of the shoe almost hit you in the face? Well, that's what happened to then President George Bush on Dec. 14, 2008 in Baghdad, Iraq.

A man identified as an Iraqi journalist named Muntuntudhar Alziadi threw his shoes at President Bush during a news conference. Bush dodged both shoes as they were thrown. Iraqis say a shoe thrown at someone is a sign of disrespect.

The history of the war between United States and Iraq begins in 1990 when Saddam Hussein attacked Kuwait. The downfall really started before that. In 1979, there was the Iraq hostage crisis. In 1983, President Ronald Reagan secretly permitted Jordon, Saudi Arabia, Kuwait and Egypt to transfer weapons to Iraq.

Will the peace stay with President Barack Obama or will relations with Iraq get worse? Only time will tell.

Niagara Falls
By Michael M.

A sixty-nine-year old crazy teacher survived going over a gigantic waterfall in a barrel. She was the first person to survive a trip over Niagara Falls. Come to Canada to try it out in a barrel.

Niagara Falls is located on the border of Ontario, Canada and New York State. There are actually three waterfalls in Niagara Falls: Horseshoe Falls, American Falls and Luna Falls.

Water from the Falls is used as hydroelectric power to make electricity. An ice jam stopped the water on Mar. 29, 1848 and people could walk out on the Falls. Today, parks and power plants are built on both sides of the Falls.

Come to Niagara Falls to have fun. Besides going over the falls in a barrel, you can hike, take a tour, shop or just relax.

Let's Discover ... Our World

Come and Visit the Beautiful Waters
By Nadya G.

Come and visit the blue waters of Fiji Islands. You can relax, get away from your kids, or bring your kids. There are beautiful hotels, cool cultures and you get to drink Fiji punch. You can go fishing in the waters and scuba dive. You have to come and visit the Fiji Islands. The people will treat you well and give you a drink when you are on an inner tube in the beautiful water.

Fiji is located in the Pacific Ocean and Australia is the closest continent. To the east is Vanuatu and to the west is Tonga. The closest island to Fiji is Tonga. Fiji is made up of 322 islands. The islands have mountains covered with tropical forests.

You should visit the Fiji Islands. The waters are so clear that you can't resist it!

Seattle, Washington
By Elle M.

Have you ever imagined what it would be like to see seals up close or be spinning while you're eating? How about walking on a volcano? If you answered "Yes" to any of these questions, visit Seattle, Washington. That is a good choice for you.

Seattle is a large city in Washington State. Washington is part of the United States. Washington is on the west coast and touches the Pacific Ocean.

The seals that are from Seattle are called harbor seals. The harbor seals are brown, tan and gray. You should not pet or disturb the seals. It's against the law!

Seattle is a really good place to see many things. Mount Rainier is a volcano in Seattle. It was formed 12 million years ago. It has many ice glaciers. People have to have special training to climb up Mt. Rainier. Also, you can visit the Space Needle. It is 607 feet high. It has a restaurant that revolves so you can see all of Seattle.

I hope you enjoy Seattle!

By Ms. Barber's Barbershop

An Adventure in Roma
By Jack W.

Did you ever want to see extreme architecture or an astonishing soccer game? Did you ever want to eat fantastic foods like pizza or spaghetti? If you like art, you'll be happy. If these are your interests, then visit Rome.

Rome is a large city located in the country of Italy. Rome is the capital of Italy. Italy is a peninsula in the Mediterranean Sea. Italy is also located in the continent of Europe.

The Romans believed in gods. They built temples and amphitheaters in honor of them. The Pantheon and Roman Coliseum are two of the most impressive monuments you can visit. The Romans built the Coliseum to entertain the gods. The Roman Coliseum is 48 meters high and measures 45 meters by 79 meters. It can hold 80,000 spectators. Sometimes the Romans would fill the Coliseum with water and have battles on boats. The Pantheon is also very impressive. The Pantheon is a temple. It was built to honor the gods Venus and Mars. It has burned down three times. Important kings of Italy are buried there.

Rome is a home to pizza and spaghetti and some of the best food in the world. Pizza is made by flattening dough, putting tomato sauce and cheese on the dough and putting it in the oven. Spaghetti is made by putting noodles in boiling water. Then, you put tomato sauce on top.

Did you know there is a country inside Rome? It's called Vatican City. It's the smallest country in the world. Rome encircles the Vatican. The Vatican is home to the Pope. The Pope's church is called the Sistine Chapel. Inside there are gorgeous paintings by the famous artist Michelangelo. The paintings are all over the ceiling.

Isn't Rome great with all its architecture and delicious food?

Let's Discover ... Our World

Fantastic Fabulous Germany
By Emma B.

Board a boat! Board a plane! Do you like chicken, pork and beef? If you do, how about visiting Germany?! Come and try their different kinds of food. I bet you would like to have a fancy breakfast, like bread and butter with chocolate spread and cold chocolate milk. They also have Kinder Eggs that are chocolate.

In Germany, their school is different than our schools in the United States. In Germany, they go to school for four years straight! Children go from kindergarten to second grade. They have to start school when they are six! They can go to the Gymnasium, which is just like high school. If you live there, you could also go to Hauptschule or Realsch to prepare for jobs to be a waitress, factory worker or mechanic. This is a good place also to learn many languages.

Germany played an important role in World War II. Adolf Hitler became the most powerful person in the German government in 1933. Six years later, he led Germany to fighting in the war. During the war, Hitler was responsible for killing millions of people, including many Jewish people. When the fighting was over in 1945, much of their country had been damaged.

If you ever want to go to Europe, go to Germany! Germany has a lot of important history you can learn. It also has a great deal of delicious food you can try. Germany would be a great place to visit!

The Wonders of New Zealand
By Libby S.

With really good weather and lots and lots of sheep, not to mention the sights, New Zealand is the place to go.

New Zealand is an island located near Australia. The biggest mountain is Mount Cook. The main islands of New Zealand are as long as the distance from San Francisco to San Diego. The North Island is hot and humid, but the South Island is quite cold. Most of the kids in the North Island have never seen snow!

The native people of New Zealand are called the Maori. They arrived from other Polynesian Islands many centuries ago. The British came later and kicked them off their lands. Today, they live modern lives but on special occasions, the Maori dress up and do the hakka, a special dance that was done to threaten opponents.

Maybe the best thing of all about New Zealand is that there is not a lot of pollution. Electric wires are underground so they don't spoil the view and the air is fresh and clean. Also, it's kind of funny that sheep outnumber people twenty to one. Another interesting fact about New Zealand is that their population eats the most ice cream in the world.

So if you're looking for a place to go with beautiful scenery, lots of ice cream and sheep, try New Zealand!

Fourth grade students used online resources including **timeforkids.com, loc.gov, nationalgeographic.com,** and **culturegrams.com** along with personal experience as sources of information for their feature/news articles.

2009 © Nottingham Elementary School

By Ms. Costa's Cardinals 4

Wonders of Colombia
By Marisa F.

Come to Colombia and eat great food, watch or play soccer anywhere and celebrate very festive holidays. It's always fun and exiting in Columbia!

The fairly small and wonderful country of Colombia is located in South America. It is nearest to the Caribbean Sea and the Pacific Ocean. Colombia is also next to Venezuela, Ecuador and close to Brazil.

In the morning, Colombian children wake up and say, "Buenos dias," to their family as they head out to school. At school, children learn science, math, history and language. Male children are always racing home from school to play soccer or basketball. Female children go home to help around the house and play dolls or talk with their friends. Colombian kids love holidays. A lot of them like *La Semana Santa* (Easter Holy Week).

The climate in Colombia is the best! Lower land temperatures are usually in the 80's (F). In higher lands, the temperatures are usually in the 50's (F). It is not too hot or too cold. Well, that's something!

Did you know Colombia is the second largest coffee producer in the world? Many people farm for a living and the majority grow coffee beans.

With so many great things to see and people to meet, you will love it in Colombia!

Sumo Wrestling in Japan
By Sam D.

Sumo wrestling is one of Japan's favorite sports. Lots of sumo wrestlers fight at National Sports Hall in Tokyo, Japan. Thousands of people crowd around to watch sumo wrestling. The ceremonies are longer than the actual competition.

S.U.M.O. stands for Sumo Ultimate Masters Organization. In ancient times, sumos fought to the death. The point of sumo wrestling is to tackle the other sumo. Sumo wrestling started as an ancient form of religion.

Sumo wrestlers eat huge meals to gain weight. Most sumo wrestlers weigh at least 325 pounds. There are even action figures of sumo wrestlers. A former sumo winner named Kaleo weighed 345 pounds. There are 70 moves that a sumo can use to get the other sumo down.

The upper division wrestlers fight in fifteen matches in each of the six tournaments in a year. The lower division wrestlers fight in seven matches. Promotions result from winning records and demotions from the opposite. At the top of the ranks are the Grand Champions and there may be one to four or more of them depending on the ability of the current wrestlers.

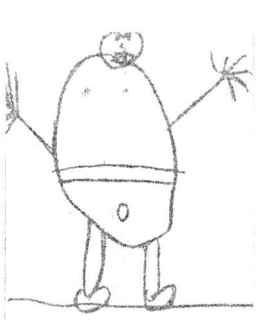

Sumo wrestling in Japan would be fun to watch because it would be cool to see sumo wrestling up close. If you want to watch sumo wrestling, it's at National Sports Hall in Tokyo, Japan!

Let's Discover ... Our World

Mad about Madagascar
By Maddie M.

Have you ever wanted to go to a wonderful, beautiful island with great warm weather and rare animals? Would you like to hear an interesting language that is actually a mix of four other languages? If so, Madagascar is the perfect place for you!

Madagascar is an island off the southeast coast of Africa. Madagascar is the fourth largest island in the world. It's almost as big as Texas! Their language is a mix of four other ones. The languages are Indonesian, African, Arabic and Malaysian. This language is called Malagasy. The first settlers were from Malaysia and Indonesia. Some of the people were from Africa and the Arabian Peninsula. These settlers came about two thousand years ago. That's why Madagascar's language is a mix of different languages.

There are lots of interesting kinds of animals in Madagascar. All of the animals are very friendly and barely any of them are afraid of humans. One of the most popular animals is the lemur. Lemurs are a lot like monkeys. One of the other very popular animals is a chameleon. There are a lot of chameleons because they like warm weather and Madagascar is very warm. The smallest chameleon is the Bookies chameleon. It is as big as your fingernail!

Now that you know about this island, go get on that airplane and fly to beautiful Madagascar!

Lifestyle in Ukraine
By Olivia Z.

Could you imagine living with ten other people in a little stuffy apartment? That's what it is like to live in Ukraine! The houses are very limited in Ukraine. That's why there are so many people living in one apartment. Many people in Ukraine are very poor.

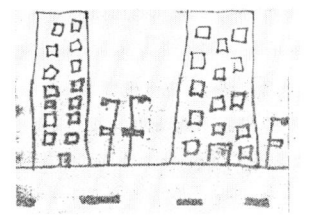

Ukraine is located in the eastern part of Europe and is a little smaller than Texas. It is located next to Romania, Belarus, Poland and Moldova. When you are in Ukraine, you are right next to the Black Sea. Right across the Black Sea is the country of Turkey. The capital of Ukraine is Kiev. The highest point is Hora Hoverla, which is 6,762 feet/2,061 meters tall. The lowest point in Ukraine is the Black Sea.

The schools in Ukraine are very challenging. You go to the same school from 1st grade to 11th grade and you have the same principal. You are in the same class all 11 years. You are required to attend school from ages six to fifteen. At the end of middle school, some children leave school to go to work, while some go on for four more years of school.

There are many different things in the Ukraine. It is much different from the United States. That's living in the Ukraine.

By Ms. Costa's Cardinals

A Kid's Life in Malaysia
By Chloe D.

Across the world, hundreds of children are in love with Speak Takraw, a sport half volleyball, half gymnastics. But where is this bizarre sport played? In Malaysia!

Malaysia is located in Asia very close to Indonesia. In fact, Malaysia even shares an island called Borneo with Indonesia.

If you were seven to ten years old living in Malaysia, this is what life might be like. In cities, kids usually live with their parents and their siblings. Many kids have to invent games to play because they are not rich enough to own fancy games. Kids only get to go to school for nine years! To get into high school, you have to take a test to see if it's worth it.

Your house in Malaysia would be built on stilts and the roof would be thatched. Homes are built this way for protection from hard rainfalls and wild animals.

When are weekends in Malaysia? In Malaysia, instead of weekends being Saturday and Sunday, their weekend is Thursday and Friday. What fun!

Now what you've been waiting for… Speak Takraw, a sport that is half volleyball, half gymnastics. Instead of using your hands to keep the ball off the ground, you use your legs, head, and chest. It's a very fast game. If you ever saw it, it would be mind blowing. Maybe you'll see it someday but for now…Selamat Tinggal! (Good bye!)

The Great Fun of Orlando
By Darren A.

Have you ever wanted to go a place with non-stop fun? Well, then Disney World in Orlando, Florida is the right place. They have spectacular rides there and they have all of the Disney characters.

A favorite ride of many visitors is Space Mountain. It looks like you're in space when you ride it. It goes about 25 miles an hour and is huge!

Some of the other rides at Disney World are: Splash Mountain, Buzz Lightyear to the Rescue, Thunder Mountain, Pirates of the Caribbean, and Space Mountain. If you like cool and fast rides, you should try Thunder Mountain and Space Mountain. If you have a baby brother, they have a lot of kiddie rides there. If you want to have some fun without your little brother, you should leave him at the kid's park with your mother. There are lots of cool roller coasters and rides at Disney World. In Disney World, they also have waterparks and good things to eat, including burgers with bacon and cheese.

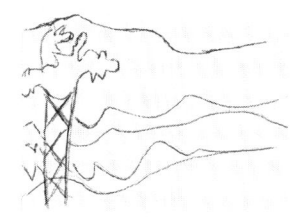

Orlando's famous sports are baseball, basketball, football, hockey, and soccer. The Orlando Magic is their professional basketball team. They play in the Amway Arena.

Other Orlando attractions include Sea World and Universal Studios. There is so much to see and do in Orlando; you will have a blast there!

Let's Discover ... Our World

Florida
By Aiden L.

Florida has a lot of beaches, warm coastal waters and lots of islands to go to. The geography of the state makes it so interesting.

Florida has one of the longest coastlines in the country. Florida is the southernmost state in the continental United States. Florida is one of the flattest states in the United States. Its highest point is only 345 feet above sea level, and many places are barely ten feet above sea level. It's difficult to imagine that billons of years ago, Florida was a series of underwater volcanic mountains, but it was. The Florida plateau separates the Atlantic Ocean from the Gulf of Mexico. Thick forests provide good homes for animals. You can also find swamps, rivers, and thousands of lakes across the state.

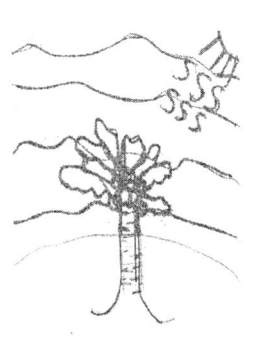

Millions of years ago, rhinoceroses, llamas, camels, pygmy horses, saber-toothed tigers and wooly mammoths roamed Florida. Today, alligators, crocodiles and four of the most poisonous snakes live within the state's border. Offshore, you can find coral reefs, playful dolphins and gentle manatees.

Florida is one of the nicest places to visit because of its great landforms and animals.

Iceland, Land of Volcanoes
By Alexis G.

December 5, 1783, Iceland

Volcanoes began erupting three weeks ago! The lava left some people homeless. The volcanoes started making earthquakes. Then the volcanoes released their tops and the lava started spitting out. People did not know when the horror would stop and they wanted to know if they should rename their homeland, Iceland, "Volcanicland" because fire was taking over the land.

Volcanoes! Volcanoes! It was a horror for all the children in Iceland. When they saw the volcanoes erupting, they thought all of their family members had died. Iceland's trees died, too. Some animals like the reindeer had also been killed.

Afterward, people thought they knew what caused the eruption. They thought that the Gods got mad at the people and made the volcanoes start to erupt.

Now the volcanoes are calming down. But most of Iceland's trees and houses are gone. Many people have lost family members and most of their homeland. But life goes on. Many of the children have been saved and checked for any broken bones and at this moment, experts are looking at the bones of the dead reindeer. Homes are being built.

Experts are looking to see what really caused the eruption. The people that lived are happy the eruptions are over and done with and life is back to normal in Iceland.

By Ms. Costa's Cardinals

Magnificent Chile
By Anna S.

Chile is a spectacular place with tons of volcanoes and delectable fruit. Chile is the longest country in the world. In fact, Chile is so long that half of Chile is cold and the other half is hot! What a wonderful place to visit!

The Portuguese sailor Ferdinand Magellan was the first European to see Chile around 1520. Chile began fighting for independence from Spain around 1810. Today, Chile celebrates its Independence Day on September 18th.

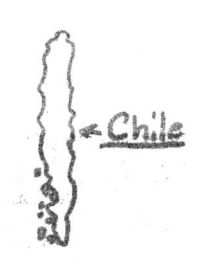

Chile is located on the west cost of South America. Chile's coastline is the Pacific Ocean. About every person in Chile likes to go to the beach to swim or fish.

Chile's flag is white, blue, red and has a star in the middle of it. The white stands for the snow of the Andes, the blue stands for the blue sky, the red stands for the blood of Chile's heroes and the star stands for progress in Chile.

Chile has about 1,080 volcanoes. The volcanoes in Chile are located in the Andes Mountains. People who live in Chile, or who are visiting Chile, like to go skiing in the Andes Mountains. Other popular sports in Chile are tennis and soccer (which they call football).

Chile is an awesome country with a lot of delicious food, cool places to visit and nice people.

Germany!
By Anton H.

Germany has nice weather, yummy food and good sports facilities. Even though we fought against the Germans in WWII, we are very good friends with them now. They have excellent chocolate and they have historic sites.

Germany is a country located in Europe. It borders the Baltic and North Seas. At one time, Germany was actually two countries – East and West Germany. But on November 9, 1989, the wall between the two countries came down and Germany became one country once again.

There are many historic sites in Germany including the Berlin Wall and numerous old castles. From kings and queens to rulers of the ages, castles have been a big part of Germany. They are tourist hot spots. They are fun to look at and go through. One of the most popular is Neuschwanstein Castle in southwest Bavaria. It was recently nominated for the new Seven Wonders of the World.

Germany's chocolate is also very famous. It is very popular in America. People like its flavor and taste. The chocolate gets its great taste from the amount of sugar and milk they put in it.

Germany's soccer team has won three World Cups and five Euro Cups. They are very good at soccer. Their logo has an eagle with a circle around it and the German flag going across their chest.

Germany is a very fun place to visit. It has one of my favorite things to eat, chocolate! I visited there last summer and hope to go back again sometime soon.

Let's Discover ... Our World

Spain
By Ben S.

Have you ever dreamed of being in the Spanish Primera, a world famous soccer league? The feel of the grass, the feel of getting slide-tackled hard? Then come over to Spain! They have awesome food and there is tons of history there! One of the most popular events in Spain is bullfighting.

Believe it or not, the first people in Spain were actually Irish. Spain shares the Iberian Peninsula with Portugal. Spain's Pyrenees Mountains form a border with France. The Balearic and Canary Islands are also part of Spain. Right now, tickets to Spain are $115 for a roundtrip. Today, Spain is a member of the European Union

As I said earlier, bullfighting is an extremely popular sport in Spain. Bullfighting works like this:

- The bullfighter steps into the arena.
- Then the bullfighter starts to wave the flag after the bull steps into the ring.

Just so you know, the bullfighter is called a president. *El Matador* in English means "The Killer." Actually, the color of the flag the bullfighter waves does not matter. It's the waving of the flag that makes the bull angry.

I think Spain is a really neat place with much to see and do. If you think it would be fun to see a bullfight, then Spain is the place for you!

Amazing Utah
By Ben Z.

Would you like to see glistening snow and breathtaking mountains? If you're not a snow kind of person, then you can go to a desert, an amusement park, a monument, or a museum. You can find all of this and more in Utah.

Utah is a state located in the western part of the United States of America. It is the second driest state in America.

Many people visit Utah to ski, including me! Some of the ski resorts located in Utah are Alta, Deer Valley, Park City and Sundance. The ski resorts are very cozy and have great rooms. The mountains are the best part, though! The powder is as thin as a piece of paper. Serious skiers consider Utah some of the best skiing in the United States!

Utah is home to many national parks. In fact, 65 percent of Utah is owned by the United States government. One of the most interesting parks is Canyonlands National Park. When you visit here, you can see canyons, sandstone needle rocks and orange cliffs. To see all these things, you would want to be a very serious hiker because there are no roads.

Utah is one of the best places to visit in the United States. Whether you like skiing or hiking, there is something amazing for you to see in Utah!

By Ms. Costa's Cardinals

Hawaii
By Carter A.

Hawaii has lots of beautiful things to see and do. Flying to Hawaii is expensive, but it is worth it. The name Hawaii comes from the Polynesian word, "*havaiki*." Havaiki means homeland or paradise. Hawaii has been the homeland of the native Hawaiian people for more than 2,000 years. It is recognized as a paradise by many others because of its incredible beauty.

No records tell when the first Hawaiians arrived. But there is evidence that people lived on the Hawaiian Islands before A.D.1. The first Hawaiians probably came from Tahiti in large canoes. Over centuries, many trips were made between Hawaii and southern Polynesia. As the population increased, kingdoms formed under high-ranking chiefs. By 1805, the islands were united under a single king-- Kamehameha 1. By that time, ships from Europe and America had reached the islands.

Hawaii's offical nickname is the "Aloha State." Aloha is a Hawaiian word that means love and affection. It is used as a greeting and farewell. The Hawaiians consider treating one another with "aloha" to be the highest form of civilized behavoir.

Hawaii is an awesome place to visit. If you go to Hawaii, you will have a fantastic time. You should live there. It is even warm year-round.

Great Islands of the Seychelles
By Davis S.

Want to come to a beautiful country for a vacation? Come to the Seychelles to have a great time! The Seychelles have a very warm climate and beautiful terrain. The beaches are one of the best parts of the Seychelles. The Seychelles also have great food and people.

The Seychelles are located on the eastern coast of Africa and right by Madagascar. The Seychelles are one of the few countries in the world to have giant tortoises. The giant tortoises are so amazing because of how big they really are.

The main sports on the island are soccer, basketball and volleyball. There are many sports leagues, especially soccer. There is also great food like spicy red snapper. The capital, Victoria, is the place to stay if you're visiting. If you want some outdoor activity, you should go to the tropical forest. It is amazing! If you want to go to the beach, this is the right place to go. There are so many interesting things to experience in the Seychelles.

The Seychelles religion is mainly Catholic, so you will see a lot of churches. If you want to learn about the Seychelles history, here is some. The Seychelles were discovered by French settlers. A lot of people in the Seychelles are very good cooks.

Ms. Pelosky really wants to go there. I wish I could go there, too.

Let's Discover ... Our World

The Holidays of Sweden
By Gabrielle E.

Different and peculiar, the holidays of Sweden contrast from the holidays of the United States. More than seven holidays are celebrated in one year, every year, in Sweden.

The country of Sweden is located at the top of Europe. The North Sea is located next to Sweden and the Arctic Circle is located to the north. Due to its northern location, Sweden has some harsh winters; so they have a huge, major, celebration when the cold weather ends. It is called the Mid-Summer which means the celebration of summer. Swedes praise summer because they have nice, warm weather. This holiday is celebrated on the June weekend which contains the longest day of the year. The Swedes decorate a pole and have a gathering. They dance and sing to show how thankful they are that summer is here.

Another interesting holiday occurs on December 13th. Swedes start Christmas by honoring their saint, St. Lucia. To honor her, a girl plays the part of St. Lucia, the light queen. She dresses in a white robe and wears a crown of candles on her head. Also on that day they eat a sweet roll called *Lussekatter*.

National Day is another special day Swedes celebrate on June 6th. On this day, they remember how Sweden won freedom so that the Danish were not ruling the Kalmar Union. That was the beginning of Sweden's independence!

Sweden definitely celebrates holidays differently than those in the United States. These holidays that I have told you about are only three of them! Swedes love these unique holidays and they bring joy to people in all of Sweden!

Astounding Israel
By Joshua R.

I am going to take you to Israel, a great place that has landscapes that range from sparkling Mediterranean beaches to striking desert landscapes.

Israel is a very small country; less than 8,000 square miles. It is located in southwest Asia on the eastern shore of the Mediterranean Sea. Israel is neighbored by Lebanon to the north, Syria to the northeast, Jordan to the east and Egypt to the southwest.

Israel has many great places to visit, including a Kibbutz, a rural community where the people share almost everything, including the money they make. There are currently about 250 Kibbutzim with 117,300 people living in a Kibbutz, in Israel.

Jerusalem is the capital of Israel. It is home to many historic places such as the Western Wall, Temple Mount and the Church of the Holy Sepulcher. Although Israel is a new country (it was founded as a Jewish sanctuary in 1948), Jerusalem is over 3,000 years old, one of the oldest cities in the world. The Western Wall is the most holy place in the world that is accessible by Jewish people because of Muslim control of the Temple Mount. Jerusalem isn't just for Jewish people; Jesus was born six miles south of Jerusalem in what is now Palestine.

So whether you're into religion, history, or just having fun, Israel is a great place to visit!

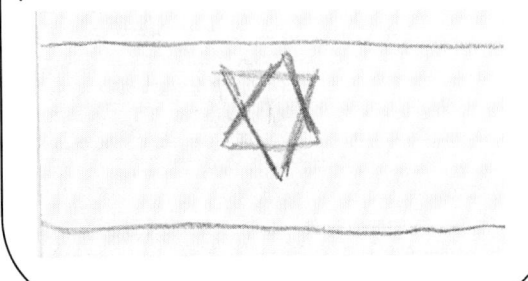

By Ms. Costa's Cardinals 4

America's Largest Oil Spill
By Kate B.

The shadow of the Exxon Valdez tank crept upon the seas of Alaska. All the animals that live there slowly awaited their fate… On that day, March 24, 1989, more than 11 million gallons of oil spilled into the ocean.

Four minutes after midnight, Joseph Hazelwood crashed the Exxon Valdez oil tank into a reef and caused a deep effect on many lives there. Oil stretched for 470 miles upon the ocean. The cost for clean up was $2.1 billion, although $125 thousand was forgiven because of the oil company's cooperation in the process. It took from 1989 to 1992 to finish the clean up. Due to the oil spill, some animals did not recover, such as the harbor seal, the Harlequin Duck, the Pacific herring and the Pigeon Quillemont.

Why was the boat there? A great amount of oil is produced in Alaska. The tank had just been loaded with North Slope crude oil.

In Alaska, fishing is very important, and after the spill, there weren't many fish left. The decrease in fish lowered the economy because it took away natural resources. The places mostly hit were Prince William Sound, the Kenai Peninsula and the Alaska Peninsula. Also some parks have been taken away from us due to the spill, including one national forest, five state parks, four critical habitat areas and a state game sanctuary.

The spill of the Exxon Valdez was the largest oil spill in America's history. Let's hope something like this never happens again!

The Rainforest Country
By Katie S.

Have you ever wanted to wake up to the sounds of chirping tree frogs, howling monkeys and the calling of toucans? Then Costa Rica is the place for you. Along with its precious wildlife, Costa Rica has thrills for everyone.

Costa Rica is a small exotic country in Central America located between Panama and Nicaragua. Many types of fascinating animals make Costa Rica their home including the easily identifiable red-eyed tree frog and the deadly strawberry poison dart frog. Some other unique animals that live in the rainforests of Costa Rica include the collard peccary, a pig-like animal that travels in small groups. While exploring the rainforest you might be lucky enough to spot the vibrant Keel-billed toucan. It has a big curved beak that is multi-colored. When it flies, its wings spread out and you can see the wonderful colors under them.

A breathtaking way to see all these animals is to take a ziplining trip. Ziplining is when you get hooked up to a cable that is strung across the trees. Then you get pushed so you soar through the trees as if you were a bird! You can choose to zipline with your family or by yourself. But no matter what type of ziplining you do, it's almost like a requirement in Costa Rica.

If any of this seems interesting to you then you should book a trip to Costa Rica today!

Let's Discover ... Our World

Life in Lithuania
By Reilly T.

When you think about the countries in Europe, you probably think of Germany or France. Well, there's one country you might not know about and it's called Lithuania.

Lithuania shares a border with Poland, Belarus and Latvia. It is only slightly bigger than West Virginia. There are 3.6 million people and most live in small families with only two or three children. If you moved there, children do the housework, so if you're a child, too bad for you!

Do you like basketball? If you do, Lithuania is the place for you! Basketball is the most popular sport there.

Lithuanians, like us, elect a president. The only difference is their president serves for five years and here, the president serves for four years.

The Lithuanian language is, of course, different from ours. So if you want to speak like a Lithuanian, here is your first lesson:

Hello = labas   (LAB-us)

Good bye = viso gero   (VIS-oh GER-oh)

Yes = taip (tape)

No = ne (neh)

I hope someday you will get a chance to explore this wonderful, lesser known European country!

The Amazing Easter Island
By Nicole K.

Have you ever wished to go to a place with sparkling beaches, palm trees, tiki statues, caves and ruins of ancient villages? Discovered by a Dutch explorer on Easter day, Easter Island is just the place to be.

Easter Island is located around 2,000 miles off of Chile in the southern Pacific Ocean. The island itself is owned by Chile. Easter Island is triangular, with an extinct volcano at each corner. The climate of Easter Island includes warm temperatures and up to 140 inches of rainfall a year.

The caves there are interesting, big, and able to be explored all over the island. The caves are rock and have a sand-gold color with a tinge of brown. The "tiki statues" are actually called Moai and hundreds are located everywhere on the island (the statues weigh around 40 tons!). The Moai are big statues with long, pointy noses. Most of the Moai statues are grouped together on stone platforms. Some of the statues are wearing hats on their heads! The hats are stone too, but their color is dirty red.

Around the island are some wild ponies. The ponies are now tame but have ancient markings on them. These ponies are descendants from the first ponies brought to Easter Island.

If you go there, you might think the land is barren and rocky, like some beaches. Other ones have beautiful turquoise waters, palm trees and glittering golden sand. Also, the water is a wonderful temperature.

With its stone statues, caves, wild ponies and beaches, Easter Island is just the place to be!

2009 © Nottingham Elementary School

By Ms. Costa's Cardinals

Guam!
By Peyton F.

Have you ever wanted to go to a place where you walk out of the plane and feel fresh, warm air? Have you ever wanted to go to a place with clear blue water and a very green jungle? Well, Guam is the place to visit!

If you go to Guam, you might see people or kids kissing each other on the cheek. You will see that because they are greeting each other.

Guam is a very small island! It is south of Japan and east of The Philippines. Guam is a territory of the United States. Guam is 30 miles long and four to eight miles wide. The main colors of Guam's flag are blue and red. Guam has many earthquakes.

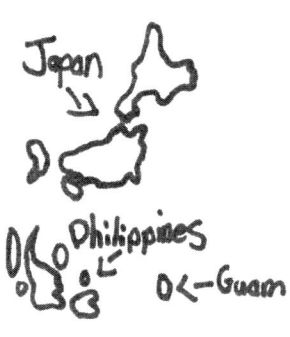

If you go to Guam, there are some buses, cars and taxis. If you want a car or any kind of transportation, never go on Sundays or holidays because there is no service!

In Guam, if you are invited to a celebration you usually will do a lot of dancing and singing. There will also be a lot of music! The banjo is Guam's favorite instrument. A lot of older men play the banjo.

People in Guam like salads and vegetables. If you are a child or a special guest, you get to go through the line of food first. Like us, Guam has three meals a day. They have breakfast, lunch, dessert time around three and they have dinner around seven.

Guam has many great things to see!

The Flood
By Sophia B.

Have you ever had a flood? If you have, you probably thought it was very bad. Then think about having three feet of water in your yard. If you were in Venice or Rome, Italy, right now, you would be experiencing the worst flood in twenty- two years!

Venice and Rome are both cities located in Italy. Italy is a country in Europe that sits on the Mediterranean Sea. Venice is located in northwestern Italy and is actually built on more than one hundred islands. It is not unusual to have a flood in Venice or Rome. It happens every year. But lately, the flooding has been unusual. In Venice and Rome, people had to wade through thigh deep water and some people had to wear plastic bags on their legs and feet to keep them dry. Lots of people got stuck in their cars and houses. One hotel was giving away free boots! People had to walk on docks for safety.

Unfortunately, the waters were dangerous. Some houses got flooded, many special possessions were lost and there was one death. The woman who died was stuck in her car while the flood waters rose. Apparently, she did not notice, and when she did it was too late. The hotels managers sent out a warning to all the visitors that they had to leave for safety. Some listened, some did not.

We hope it will not happen again.

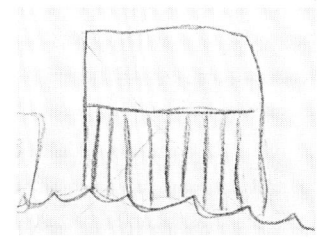

2009 © Nottingham Elementary School

Let's Discover ... Our World

Pompeii
By Emma H.

Have you ever wanted to go to a place where a volcano erupted? Where you can see people that are covered in cement? Well, there is a place like that and it's called Pompeii!

When Mt. Vesuvius erupted, rock and ash shot into the air like fire. When you go there today there are people that died and are preserved in the ash. The preserved people were covered with cement that was nearly 30 feet thick.

Pompeii was rediscovered by a peasant digging a well. Pompeii is located in southern Italy right near Naples. Pompeii was lost for about 1,700 years until 1748 when it was rediscovered! Pompeii is a very cool place today! When you walk around the streets you will see artifacts like all the ash-covered people.

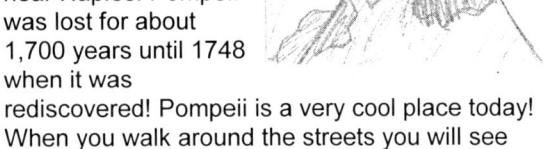

Tourists of Italy come to Pompeii a lot. In 2008, there were 2.6 million tourists in Pompeii ... that's a record! Pompeii is a very popular place today!

You should go to Pompeii to see history. If you go there, you could tell people that you have been to a place with lots of history and a place where a volcano erupted! Your friends will be shocked! So plan a trip and go there today!

Sweden
By Aidan H.

Did you ever want to explore rocky coasts on a far out country? If so, you should visit Sweden!

Sweden is a rocky country in the northeastern part of Europe. It is bitter cold in the winter. It is a place perfect for skiing. Sweden is one tenth bigger than California. It's amazing! Sweden borders Finland and Norway. Sweden has a low population for such a big place. Sweden has a form of government called a *constitutional monarchy*. Constitutional monarchy is another term for a government led by kings and queens.

Did you know that the Nobel Peace Prize is awarded in Sweden each year? Sweden also has many cool historic sites and a few castles which are pretty amazing. Sweden has a lot of farm land. Most cities are highly populated in the northern part of Sweden. They also get over two feet of snow each year.

Sweden has a popular soccer team and they also play a little cricket. People from Sweden often compete in the Olympics. Sweden has a tough terrain on the coasts, which is great for experienced cyclists.

Sweden has many cool things but I'm going to let you figure out the rest. It will be challenging. Good luck!

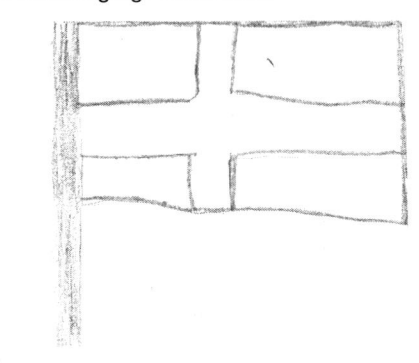

Fourth grade students used online resources including **timeforkids.com, loc.gov, nationalgeographic.com,** and **culturegrams.com** along with personal experience as sources of information for their feature/news articles.

By Ms. Matthews' Mariners

4

The Netherlands
By Kathryne S.

Have you ever wondered what wooden shoes feel like? Have you ever wondered what the Dutch language sounds like? Well, here's my opinion . . . you should go to the Netherlands!

The Netherlands are located in the northwestern part of Europe bordering Germany. People often call the Netherlands, "Holland," but that is incorrect. In the Netherlands people speak Dutch. William the Silent was the leader of the Netherlands during the Dutch Revolt. They founded a republic in 1581. The capital of the Netherlands is Amsterdam. The population of the Netherlands is 16,645,313 people. Wow!!!

The Netherlands has some pretty unique clothes! There is a type of headgear that's called a *chaperon*. It was a form of hood and it is worn all over the western part of Europe. There is a cap that's called a *Dutch cap* and it is worn for Dutch costumes. There are shoes that came from the Netherlands and those are wooden shoes but can be called *clog shoes*. and these shoes are made from wood. My opinion is that wooden shoes aren't very comfortable!

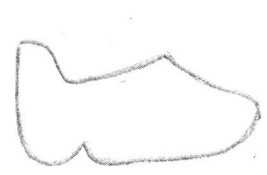

I think the Netherlands would be an awesome place to visit and live. The history is very interesting and what I wrote down is not even close to everything that has happened in the Netherlands! You'll love it if you go there!

China's Pandas
By Catherine W.

Do you like pandas and Chinese food? Then come to China and visit the Chinese Zoo!

China has giant pandas. Some giant pandas live in Chinese forests. Those pandas are called wild pandas. In 2007, the Chinese zookeepers found the wild pandas and took them to the zoo.

When a female panda is having a baby, she needs lots of privacy. When panda babies are born, they can weigh up to 3 pounds! They can also be as big as a stick of butter.

Pandas can eat bamboo non stop! Some pandas can actually swim. It's hard to believe, but it is true! Come to China and look for the Chinese Zoo, then look for the pandas.

Chinese food is also important in China! All their restaurants are filled with Chinese food. Some of the snacks are spicy and some are sweet. There are spicy noodles, rice and chicken. Their main food is, obviously, rice.

There are lots of Chinese restaurants in America, so go to one now!

Let's Discover ... Our World

Australia
By Matthew N.

Did you ever want to visit a place where animals roam at every corner? If you said yes, then Australia is the place for you! Australia is in the southeast hemisphere. It's called, "Down Under."

Australia has over 700 types of birds! One of the 700 types of birds is the rainbow lorikeet. Australia is also the home to the Tasmanian devil. Some people even train dolphins and orcas to do tricks! The echidna can live to be 50 years old. Australia has 50 different types of kangaroo. Some even climb rocks and the bush baby has HUGE eyes to see well at night. The Great Barrier Reef in Australia is one of the biggest reefs in the world and has many different kinds of fish. One of them is the crown-of-thorns starfish. It eats the reef.

The cane toad was brought to Australia. Once a dog ate one and they are poisonous. Luckily, he survived. The Tasmanian Devil I told you about earlier is losing population. It's related to the kangaroo because it too has a pouch. So that's Australia!

Cambodia
By Laura C.

Have you ever wanted to visit a place with a bunch of cities, water, cool architecture and a lot of rich history? Then Cambodia is the place for you!

Cambodia is in southeast Asia, right between Thailand, Vietnam and Laos.

Ankor what? No, Ankor Wat. You can go sightseeing there. It has an amazing temple. The temple has four points on the roof and is mostly tan. It is so incredible that it's on the Cambodian flag. The word *Ankor* comes from the Khmer word for temple.

Some cities to go to in Cambodia are Battambang, Kratie, Kamport, Poipet, Pursat, Siem Reap, Sisophon, Takeo and the capital, Phnom Pen.

If you want to see many amazing sights, plan your visit to Cambodia today!

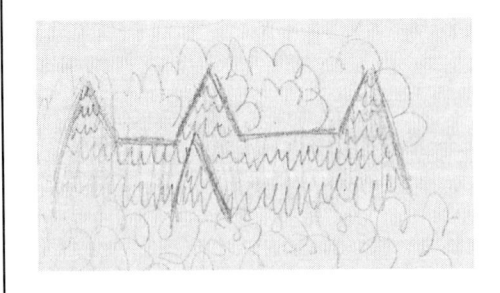

2009 © Nottingham Elementary School

By Ms. Matthews' Mariners

Canary Islands
By Anna F.

Have you ever wanted to go to a beach where the sun is always shining? Where the calm ocean waves lap up against the rocks on the beach? Then any one of the seven Canary Islands is the place for you!

DUST STORMS
On March 10, 2007, thick plumes of dust blew off the west coast of Africa and over the Canary Islands. The sea water appeared green under the dust. A wall of Sahara desert dust was captured in a photo.

DID YOU KNOW?
Did you know that in 1492 Christopher Columbus stopped in the Canary Islands with the Pinta, the Nina and the Santa Maria? After five weeks he left and continued on his journey.

ABOUT THE CANARY ISLANDS
The Canary Islands are small, beautiful islands off the coast of Africa. The Canary Islands are very hot, yet relaxing. The Canary Islands are spectacular islands with luxurious hotels and fun activities for your kids to enjoy. I would recommend going! Because the Canary Islands are the best and most beautiful islands I've ever been to! I bet your wondering how I've been to the Canary Islands, right? Well, I lived in London for two years so I had the chance to go to the Canary Islands.

Rome
By Tim W.

Rome is the biggest city in Italy. Italy is a country in Europe. Rome has the finest of a lot of things like food and sculptures. They even have one of the finest in the soccer teams!

Some of their best foods in Rome are pasta, pizza, risotto (Italian rice), gelato (Italian ice cream), lasagna, bread and olive oil. Some famous Roman architecture includes the Coliseum where the gladiators used to fight and the Trevi fountain. Both are a big part of history.

Some of Rome's good soccer teams are A.C. Milan which includes famous players such as David Beckham, Ronaldo, Kaka, Ronaldinho, and Maldini (who I think retired). Another team, Roma, is home of Totti, a very famous player, and Italy, the national team.

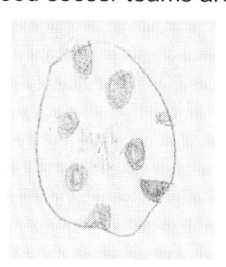

Rome is located in Italy, in Europe close by the Mediterranean Sea. Italy is on a peninsula. North of Rome is Milan, the capital of Italy. Most people think that Rome is the capital, but Rome is just the biggest city, not the capital. Rome is also home of the Vatican which is actually its own small country.

You would want to visit Rome because they have interesting history that is fascinating! If you're a big soccer fan or a food lover, you should go there!!!! The ruins of Rome are really cool!

Let's Discover ... Our World

The City is Sinking!
By Megan G.

The city is sinking and it's sinking pretty fast. Two and a half inches per decade, that's how fast it's sinking. Venice is that city. It is in Italy which is located in Europe. Italy is on the Mediterranean Sea.

Flooding in Venice is nothing new; there have been high tides since the sixth century. Alarms sound when high tides hit Venice. The alarms usually sound in fall or winter. The biggest tide hit Venice on November 4, 1996. Scientists think that in one hundred years, the water level will rise between seven inches and two feet.

The Venice government is trying to help. Since 2003, they have been building floodgates called MOSE. They say MOSE will be finished in 2012. They are putting up barriers at three inlets where the Adriatic Sea meets the lagoon. Even if, the floodgates break, it will give scientists plenty of time to figure out what to do. When a high tide comes, air will pump up MOSE and it will start blocking the water.

I think Venice is sinking because of global warming. The ice caps in the Arctic Ocean are melting and when they melt the water level rises and I think all that water is splashing into Venice.

Burkina Faso
By Mary Elliott A.

Do you like the name Ouagadougou? Then you should visit Burkina Faso, and the capital, Ouagadougou.

Burkina Faso is located in Western Africa, north of Ghana. To give you a feel of how big the country is, it is slightly larger than Colorado. The population is 15,264,735.

If you go outside in the winter, Burkina Faso is tropical, warm and dry. If you go outside in the summer, it is hot and wet. If you go there on August 5, they will be celebrating their Independence Day from France. If you go on December 11, they will be celebrating Republic Day.

There is not much to do in Burkina Faso because they only have three TV stations: two private and one national. It is really hard to get to Burkina Faso because they only have three airports that are paved. If you go there, you might want to look for some of their natural resources like limestone, marble and small deposits of gold.

So they next time you visit Africa, go to Burkina Faso.

By Ms. Matthews' Mariners

Three of Australia's Unique Animals
By Emma P.

Have you ever thought of a place where you could see a platypus, bush baby and a kangaroo? Well, there is such a place. This place is Australia!

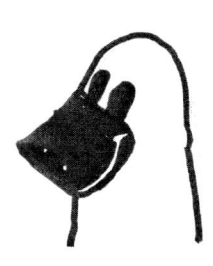

Have you ever thought of an animal that had a duck bill, otter feet and a beaver tail? The platypus is a semi-aquatic egg-laying mammal. The platypus is one of a few venomous mammal species. The platypus is on the Australian 20 cent coin. Also, in the 20th century, they were hunted for their fur. Their body is coated in brown fur to keep it warm. The platypus actually has a rubbery snout instead of a bill.

Have you ever thought of having a name that makes you seem like you were born in a bush? Also known as Galagos, Bush Babies are small nocturnal primates who are good leapers and run swiftly. Their diet is insects, small animals, fruit and tree gums.

Kangaroos are marsupials. Wild ones were once shot for meat, for sport and to protect grazing areas for sheep and cattle. The kangaroo is the national symbol for Australia. They have powerful hind legs to jump and large feet adapted for leaping and a long, muscular tail for balance.

I hope these unique animals don't become extinct anytime soon.

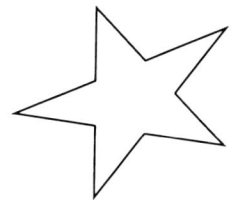

Germany's History in the 1900's
By John P.

The history of Germany in the 1900's was interesting. A war broke out and the German army was in the middle of it. Later another war broke out and the German army was at it again. World Wars I and II were bad wars to be in. Living was harsh and cold in the winters. Some people in London or Tokyo were lucky to live. In Nagasaki and Hiroshima not many people survived. At the time of World War II, Germany had a horrible leader that randomly killed Jewish people and then killed himself when he knew he would be captured.

Later Russia (Soviet Union) took over half of Germany and Berlin, Germany's capital city. The other half of Germany and Berlin was occupied by the United States of America, United Kingdom and France. The Soviets built a wall to keep people in West Berlin from escaping. Eventually the wall came down and Germany was free once again. There are many cool places you could visit like Berlin, and maybe you could get a piece of the wall!

Germany is located in central Europe. It has 11 borders, nine from other countries and two from seas. Germany is a nice place to go if you like the country. It also is the place to go if you like noisy cities. Germany is the place to be.

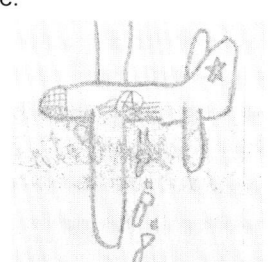

Let's Discover ... Our World

Interesting Italy
By Danielle W.

Do you like pasta? If you do, Italy is the place for you to eat. Have you ever wondered what it's like to be a kid in Italy? Did you know that kids in Italy go to school six days a week but they only have five hours of school each day?

People in Italy usually have a pasta course in midday. The type of pasta you eat in Italy depends on where you live. Did you know that kids in Italy only wear their tennis shoes in the gym or on the athletic fields?

In northern Italy, people cook seafood, shellfish and pasta. Also in northern Italy they make flat ribbon-shaped pasta with cream sauces. Southern Italy makes their pasta with macaroni and tomato-based sauce. Wine in Italy is usually served with every meal except breakfast. Popular meats they eat are veal and pork. People in Italy also like cheese.

If you go to school in Italy you can go to elementary or primary school. Primary school is for kids ages six to 11 and it lasts about five years. In Italy, kids go for a usual family walk on Sunday. Some of the games children in Italy play are basketball, soccer, Formula 1 racing and bocce ball, which is a very old Italian tradition. They speak Italian in school but they do learn English.

Stop by Italy any time!

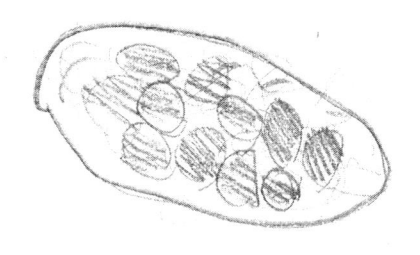

Japan's Animals
By Sydney D.

Come and see Japan. Japan has lots of cool animals.

Snow monkeys are native to Japan. Did you know snow monkeys raided some stores? Have you ever been to Japan? Have you ever seen a snow monkey? They're so cute. Did you know snow monkeys love ponds? They jump and swim everywhere in them.

Another interesting animal is a marine mammal called a dugong. It lives in the sea and eats fish. It has a circle mouth. It's like a vacuum.

Another animal that used to live in Japan was a sea lion. People believe Japanese sea lions became extinct in the 1950's. They were related to the California sea lion. In case you did not know, a sea lion has four flippers. It has whiskers. Sea lions love fish. (I don't think they eat anything else but fish.) Sea lions look a little like a seal.

Come to Japan and see cool animals any time!

By Ms. Matthews' Mariners

Argentinean Foods
By Rachel C.

Do you like meat, especially beef? Are cattle your favorite animal? If you do or they are, Argentina's the place for you. If there are any vegetarians or vegans reading this, I do not recommend you go to Argentina.

Argentina's official name is Argentine Republic. It is in South America. Its capital is Buenos Aires. They speak Spanish. Its border countries are Uruguay, Brazil, Paraguay, Bolivia and Chile. Some of its cities are: Córdoba, Bahía Blanca, Paraná, Tucumán and Rosario. One of its landmarks is Palacio Fuentes in Rosario.

Argentina is one of the world's major food producers. They produce a lot of meat (especially beef), wheat, corn, milk, beans and soybeans. Red meat is common. Argentina's annual consumption of beef averaged 220 lbs per capita. Argentinean's have a high protein diet.

Large amounts of domestically-harvested wheat are used to make white bread (made with white flour). Wheat-based Italian dishes are popular such as pizza. Tomatoes, onions, lettuce, eggplant, squashes, and zucchini are common sides.

Here are some Argentinean dishes:
Asado- barbecued meats
Chorizo- pork sausage
Chinchulines- chitterlings
Morcilla- blood sausage
Mollejas- sweetbread
Chivito- goat
Chimichurri- sauce of herbs, garlic, and vinegar
Schnitzel- breaded and fried meat
Alfajores- Argentinean version of tea pastries
Milanesas- meat dish as snack

And remember, if you like meat and cattle, you should go to Argentina!

Let's Discover ... Our World

Tibet and Protests
By Isabel Z.

If there is a place in the world where you might not want to visit right now, it would be Tibet. If you were going to choose between going on a train for a month or going to Tibet, I would choose being on a train for a month because Tibet is having a really big problem with protesting. The Tibetans want their "state" back.

Once Tibet was its own independent kingdom but today it is part of the People's Republic of China. The flag of Tibet was used between 1912 and 1920. It was introduced by the 13th Dalai Lama in 1912. The Chinese attacked Tibet in the 1950's so some of the Tibetans moved to Nepal and now live there. They also protest there to get their own country to not be under Chinese ruling. There used to be a lot of monks in Tibet but most moved and now live in Nepal.

Tibet is a high, wind-swept plateau, with bitterly cold winters and short cool summers. On the border between Tibet and Nepal stands Mount Everest, the world's highest mountain.

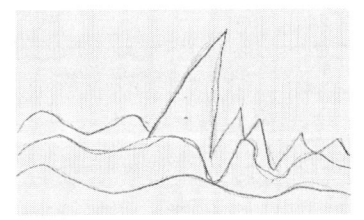

Protests
Tibetans current protest to get their state back has been the biggest since the 1980s. The Chinese said they would deal harshly with the protests if they keep going. They accused the Dalai Lama, the spiritual leader of the Tibetan Buddhists, of mastering the protests. One thousand Tibetans sacrificed their lives but it has not helped.

Buddhist monks are calling for the release of other imprisoned monks. They were soon joined by other Tibetans. After ten hours of protests, the Chinese sprayed them with tear gas.

Amazing Chinese Pandas
By Erik T.

Have you ever seen Chinese pandas in the zoo? You probably have. If you like seeing them in the zoo, you should see them in the wild. Wild pandas eat more than 40 pounds of bamboo a day! It is rare to see a giant panda in the wild so you are lucky if you see one! The forests where the wild pandas live are near Beijing, China.

In the Olympics this past year, 12 panda cubs were the Asian country's mascots. The cubs raised lots of money for the Chinese zoo where the pandas live. The money will be used for good care, doctors and good food for the pandas.

The bad part is that only about 1,600 pandas are left. Now humans are doing all they can to help the pandas. If you like pandas, China is the place to be.

By Ms. Matthews' Mariners

Italy
By Sirak G.

Have you wondered why people fought to death in the Coliseum? Well, they were gladiators. In ancient Rome, if you were not a citizen or if you were a slave or a burglar, you were probably going to become a gladiator. If you fought for eight years the king might let you be a citizen. There were three types of battles in the Coliseum: land wars, sea wars, and animal wars. Rome has a lot of history.

Rome is a large city located in Italy. Italy is a country in Europe.

Italians eat bread, pizza, pasta, Nutella and gelato.

Italy has a lot of history. I hope you get to go to Italy.

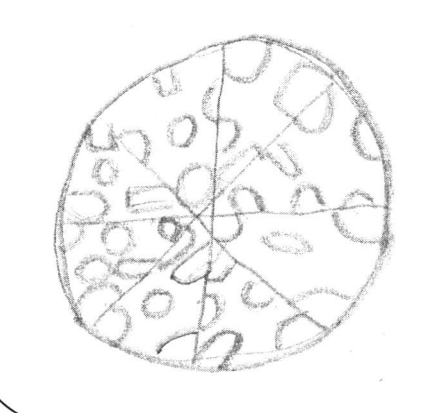

Tombs, Stone Circles, and Castles, Oh My
By Elizabeth W.

If you are looking to go to a place where there is never-ending excitement, lots of interesting things to do and medieval and historic things to visit and see, Cork, Ireland is the place for you!

Cork, Ireland is a very busy city. Cork is the largest of the Irish cities. Cork is a great place to visit because it has such wonderful things to see; from dolmens (chamber tombs) and stone circles, to ruins of medieval abbeys and churches and, of course, the Blarney Castle!

The Blarney Castle was originally a timber hunting lodge in the 10th century. When you enter the castle, that is made of a grey stone, it feels cold, damp, and mysterious!

The world famous Blarney Stone is situated high up in the battlements of the castle. You can acquire the gift of eloquence by kissing the stone. Warning: there is only one way to get to the stone: upside down and backwards. Almost like doing a backbend! I guarantee you will remember that moment forever and ever more! Don't worry there is a keeper of the stone, to support you and lower you down!

Come and see the castle for yourself, and you too can acquire the gift! Cork is only a plane ride away, so come today!

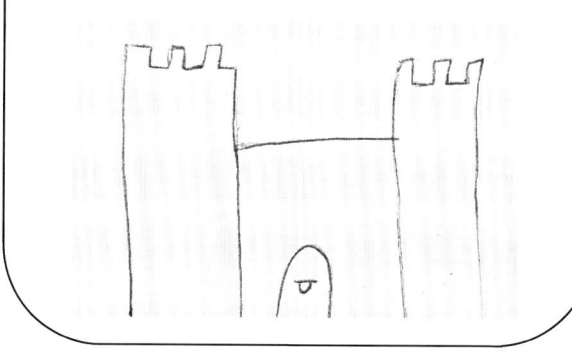

Let's Discover ... Our World

The Land of Fire and Ice
By R.K. K.

Have you ever wanted to go to a place that geologists, volcanologists, and scientists call "amazing," "spectacular" and "a geologic wonder"? Now you can and it's only five hours from New York. Iceland is also known as, "The Land of Fire and Ice" with many spas and hotels. Iceland is a great place for exploring where you will never be bored.

Iceland is amazing for many reasons. Iceland has the northern most capital in the world. It is an island made entirely of lava rock. 99.9% of Iceland's electricity is currently generated from renewable resources such as geothermal energy. WOW! Because the whole country is **almost** going bankrupt, it might not be a good idea to go to Iceland right now. Although if you are bored, go to Iceland and don't forget to spend your money. Help them out of bankruptcy if you do go. (No; I don't work for Iceland).

Arlington National Cemetery
By Hayden K.

Do you know what the biggest graveyard is? Arlington National Cemetery has 420 acres and 60,000 graves which makes it **HUGE**. It was the house of Robert E. Lee of the Confederate army. There are more then 3,800 Civil War soldiers, 24 British soldiers, 5 Canadian soldiers, 4 Italian soldiers, and 19 astronauts buried at Arlington National Cemetery! If you want to learn more, keep reading!

Arlington National Cemetery is located in Arlington, Virginia in the United States of America.

They have sections in the cemetery so if someone is looking for a dead person they know where to find them. The graves are numbered for the same reason that the sections exist: to help people find a specific person.

The Arlington National Cemetery is a great place to visit because you can see the graves of men and women from all over the world. There might be one of your dead relatives buried there. It is a pretty place, so go visit it now!

By Ms. Matthews' Mariners

All About the Gods of Egypt
By Lizzy T.

Would you like to go to a place where you can learn about the funny names gods have and the stories the Egyptians had for them? You'll see gods and goddesses pictured on the walls of tombs and buildings. If you want to do that kind of stuff, Egypt is the place for you to go!

Egypt is located in northeast Africa, near the Mediterranean Sea and the Red Sea.

A long time ago, a sand pile was in the middle of the sea. On the pile, was the first god of Egypt, Atum. He soon found Shu, the god of air, and Tefnut, the goddess of moisture. Tefnut and Shu had two kids, Geb, god of earth and Nut, goddess of sky. Nut and Geb had four kids, Osiris, Isis, Seth and Nephthys. Osiris and Isis got married and had a kid named Horus.

Stories of a pharaoh's life were written on the walls of tombs for use in the underworld, the kingdom of Osiris. Known Egyptian history is 2,600 years long. Gods had a role to play in keeping peace and order. Some brought floods, some protected people and others had important jobs, too.

If the Egyptians had not made tombs and temples for their gods and pharaohs, we may not know anything about them today! If you visit Egypt, you can see them for yourself.

Italy
By Patrick G.

Italy is in Europe. Italy is home to the Coliseum, which is where gladiators used to fight in games. We admire it today. The nice thing about Italy is that the people in Italy are so nice and caring. In Italy, some families have up to ten people.

If you go to Italy, they have transportation by car, metro or bus. Italy is very beautiful and has lots of sights to see, including art. Michaelangelo was an artist who created sculptures that were naked. Back then, this type of art was considered great.

Italy has the best food ever. One type of food is a chocolate also known as Nutella. Nutella is very good. They have meals that have pasta and bread. Their food is delicious. Gelato is also a very good food that Italy is known for making. Did you know that in Italy, when wine spills on something, it is good luck to put it behind your ear?

That is why we admire Italy today because of all the scenery and food. That's why I chose Italy.

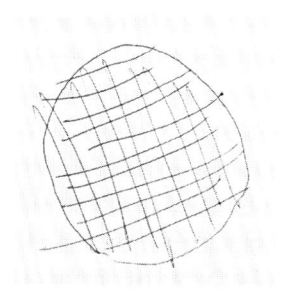

Let's Discover ... Our World

They Call Their Parents "Oldies"
By Nicholas M.

Where in the world can you go to see kiwis saying funny words? New Zealand!

New Zealand Is located southeast of Australia, between the Tasman Sea and the South Pacific Ocean. It is 103,737 square miles or about the size of Colorado. Its capital is Wellington.

The natural resources of New Zealand are natural gas, coal and hydropower. The commercial resources are gold, iron ore, limestone, sand and timber.

If you plan to go to New Zealand, you should visit Auckland. It's the largest city and you can see the tallest building in the southern hemisphere. It's called the Auckland Sky Tower and it is 1,076 feet tall! Auckland is between two coasts and is said to have the most pleasure boats per person in the world! It would be very fun to visit Auckland!

New Zealand was the first country to give women the right to vote. It was in 1893, while in America they didn't let women vote until 1920. Way to go, New Zealand!

People talk kind of funny in New Zealand. They speak English but with a sort of a British accent. The other language New Zealanders speak is Maori. They call their parents, "Oldies". Their word for sunglasses is "sunnies". Their word for candy is "lollies". Their word for hello is "G'day." They also have some other different words, like, "Dunny," "Jandals," "Ta," "Snarlers" and "Rellies." I am not going to tell you what they mean. You will have to go to New Zealand to find out.

The people from New Zealand are called "Kiwis". So next time you're in the southern hemisphere, go to New Zealand and say, "G'day" to a Kiwi!! New Zealand is awesome!

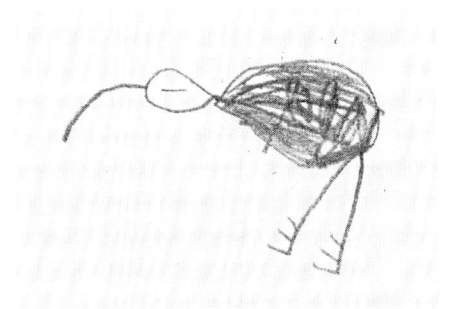

By Ms. Matthews' Mariners

Magnificent Animals
By Patrick W.

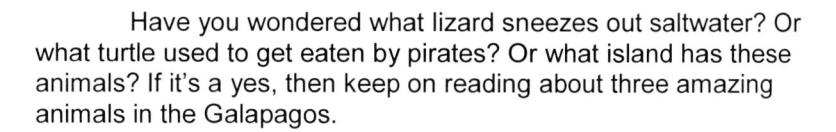

Have you wondered what lizard sneezes out saltwater? Or what turtle used to get eaten by pirates? Or what island has these animals? If it's a yes, then keep on reading about three amazing animals in the Galapagos.

The Galapagos Islands are 13 islands located about 600 miles off the coast of Ecuador in South America. They were created by underwater volcanoes millions of years ago. Now people live on four of the islands.

The blue-footed booby the most distinguishable bird in the Galapagos. Their wingspan is about 25-36 inches. More than 70% of the booby population can be found in the Galapagos. The other 30% can be found in other places such as California and Colorado!

Another unique animal that calls the Galapagos home is the marine iguana. It is the only sea-going lizard in the world! They eat algae under water. They are expert divers and swimmers and can hold their breath up to an hour! They pile up on lava rocks to rest, keep warm and sneeze out saltwater, which gives them a white hairdo.

The giant tortoise is the main symbol of the Galapagos. They are the largest tortoises in the world often weighing over 400 pounds and living to be 150 years old! You can't see how old they are by counting their rings. The tortoises lives on seven of the thirteen islands. They eat grasses, leaves, herbs, flowers, fruit and fallen cactus pads. A long time ago pirates, and sailors used to eat them and that's why they are endangered.

The Galapagos is a really cool place that has even more amazing animals and amazing features. You should plan to visit there some day!

My Incredible Imagination

The Thunder Storm
By Amy B.

pitter-patter, pitter-patter,
pitter-patter, pitter-patter,
pitter-patter, pitter-patter,
drip-drop, drip-drop,
drip-drop, drip-drop,
drip-drop, drop-drop,
thunder, lightning,
thunder, lightning,
thunder, lightning.
drip-drop, drip-drop,
drip-drop, drip-drop,
drip-drop, drop-drop,
pitter-patter, pitter-patter,
pitter-patter, pitter-patter,
pitter-patter, pitter-patter,
Shhh!

Words Are Like…
By Audrey H.

Words are like cats,
Lying low, waiting
For the perfect moment
To capture your imagination.

Words are like
A soft breeze
Loftily floating into your head
Or a storm wind
Forcing you to believe the unbelievable.

Words are like
A butterfly
Fluttering freely from your fingers.
A bird chirping
Singing its song of happiness.

Words can be warm and soft,
Happy and free,
Making your heart feel the lightest of all.

Words can be
Dark and hard,
Cold and harsh,
Making your mind cloud with fear.

Words make you feel many different things…
Sadness, hope, joy, courage, and fear.
But they are all the same,
All words.

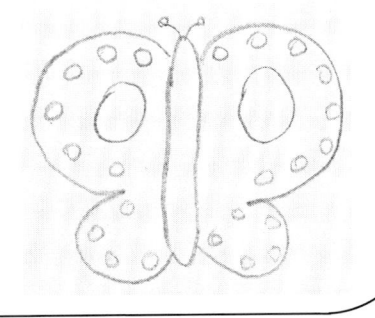

Disclaimer: As part of the writing process, fifth graders were encouraged to explore their imagination through poetry. Students learned how poets use sensory details to express their creativity and how they frequently break the rules of grammar on purpose. Therefore, their poems may or may not adhere to proper usage rules.

2009 © Nottingham Elementary School

By Ms. Ashley's Smarties   5

Bouncing Soccer Ball
By Brandon W.

If you are a soccer player
  You can hear everybody on your team
 Prancing back
And forth
  Shooting the ball.
Feeling a sudden power go through you
Opening your eyes you can see a dog pile on you
Leaping
 Everywhere
 Noticing that you scored a goal.
The grass is all green.
 The goal is all white.
       You still see the ball
            Still rolling in the goal.

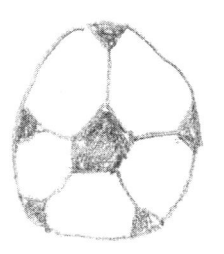

I Don't Know What To Do!
By Austin C.

I don't know what to do, do, do.

We're gonna have a test, test, test.

I watched TV, V, V, V

On my DVD, D, D, D.

I forgot to study, study, study, study.

So I guessed, guessed, guessed, guessed.

The test is finally over, over, over.

What a relief, lief, lief, lief.

What is that I hear?

A test the very next week!!!

My Incredible Imagination

November
By Diana L.

Breezes coming and going
Plus blowing.
Chilly
Willy,
Weather is here or near.
Now if it's
Chilly
Willy,
It's down
To the
Bound
Breezes
White bright,
Frost on the,
Down to the ground.
Inside Warm
Of a,
Swarm,
Of
Apple pies baking.
Leaves falling,
Plus swifting
To the so,
Bound ground.
Trees close, or
Definite
Bare to the snare.

The sounds
Of
Scrunching,
Crunching,
Bunching,
Leaves fill the air.
Leaves are shifting, to
The bound ground.
Leave piles shifting,
Down the Breet Street.

Sold cold fills the,
Bare air,
As brisk as Swiss.
Bitter nitter
Snow is on the
Bays Way.
Warm and cold,
But fall
Brings it all.
Fall is
Coming and going
But November is still here.

THERE'S ONLY ONE OCTOBER
By Joe D.

The *crack* of the bat,
The roar of the crowd,
The people fight for the ball in the streets,
After it goes over the titanic scoreboard.

The *crack* of the bat,
The sight of the dirt springing happily in the air,
The ball hits a glove with a *thwack*,
The spectacular throw to first,
Next, only the sweet sound of,
"He's out!" from the ump.

With two strikes,
The wind-up, and the hurl,
"Strike three!" you hear from the ump,
Next you're blacked out,
When you wake-up,
You're at the bottom of a dog pile,
Crowned the World Champions.
That's why there is only one October.

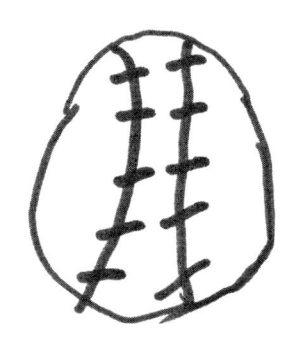

By Ms. Ashley's Smarties

5

Springing Into Spring and Summer
By Kelly E.

Spring, spring,
Breezy and warm

I frolic in green bud filled meadows
With only a long sleeve shirt and pants.

My winter coat has retired
Along with its friends, hat, gloves, and scarf.

Blossoms are blooming
Gardens are becoming more vivid.

Easter went by as fast as a cheetah,
Along with all of the chocolate.

Chirp chirp tweet tweet sing the birds advancing home
Other animals are coming out.

Sports are now starting
My birthday is sooner
Rain is more common as well.

Summer is approaching
Warmth is coming to town.

Shorts and a T-shirt are
What I am currently wearing
School is starting to conclude.

Summer, summer,
Scorching and sizzling.

I Hate Poetry
By Katherine L.

I hate poetry.
I just don't get it.
The teacher likes it,
I don't.

I hate poetry.
I hate to rhyme.
It just wastes time!

I hate poetry.
It just isn't fun.
What's wrong with normal writing?

I hate poetry.
We do it every year!
Writing would be my favorite subject
If it wasn't for poetry!!!

I hate poetry.
It's like dead fish!
Do you see why I hate it?
It stinks!

Wait a second!
What am I doing?
I'm writing a poem!!!
NOOOOOO!!!!!

My Incredible Imagination

DECEMBER
BY LAUREN G.

The delicate soft snow
calmly falling
like the rain
but slower and quieter.

The sun
glistening against
the snow,
as it slowly
melts.

Watching the
exhilarated kids play
in the snow.

The beautiful sound of
kids cheering,
the crunching
and slurping
of people eating
cookies and drinking
hot chocolate.

The wonderful
smell of
fresh baked cookies
and hot chocolate
being stirred.

The delicate
soft snow,
the glistening sun,
the hot chocolate,
the fresh baked cookies,
and the kids
having fun.

The Poem That Doesn't Make Sense
By Matt F.

My name is Matt.
I do not have a pet rat.
I have an old dog named Zoey
And an Auntie named Joey.

I have splat on my hat and rocks in my socks.
My room is usually clean
But sometimes it shouldn't be seen.
The word *moo* is from a cow
And I like the band named the Who.
When I play the drums,
My mom eats Tums.
I don't like mooshie in my sushi,
But I love sushi.

I got my dad from a T.V. ad.

The last time I saw my vicious sister,
She was mixed up in a game named Twister.

When I played baseball, my ball went through a wall.
They made a call and I felt very tall.

My name is Matt and you've heard all that.
This is the end until we meet again.

By Ms. Ashley's Smarties

January
By Michael H.

The New Year has approached the old year can go, a
 New spring
Awaits us deep
In the snow.

It's the
Middle
Of winter,
Chills in the air,
Temperature falling
All through the air… freezing
Our toes but shun as it nips your
Nose.

In joy to the snowflakes falling to the ground
Dancing
Around and around.

Slowly the
Snow
Will rise
Until I am covered
Up to my eyes.

January the best month of
All.

The old year can go, it is time for the
New year to show.

Jib Jib Jot
By Natalie P.

A Jib Jib Jot with a Trot
A Jib Jib Jib Jot
What a thought
A big furry dot

What? A ut A big big ut.
Shiny sword cut cut cut.
No more ut

A Jib Jib Jot to the yacht
Big Big yacht
A Jib Jib jot
Zib Zib Zot!

My Incredible Imagination

Blaze
By Nick M.

In
December
A
Tiny
Glowing
Orange
Ember
Falls on the
Tinder
And Ignites
The Fire Rages

Crackles

Burns

Then
Out
By
A
Splash
With
A
Wisp
It's
Gone

Splish
By Noelie Z.

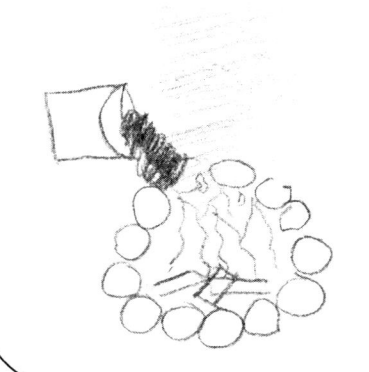

Splish,

Splash every

Second. Squeak on

The bottom of feet running

All around the yard. Auhh, auhh says

The open mouths trying to catch a drop.

Spit splat kaboom jump into the little brown hole

Collecting drip drop until full jump, refill, jump,

Refill until splash halts but squeak one more

Time while everyone walks inside. The rain is

Gone but the fun is not for after spring rain

Comes summer hot. While summer brings swimming

And ice cream we will be awaiting another

Rainy day the following year.

By Ms. Ashley's Smarties 5

LADYBUGS
BY SOFIA C.

A black spotted thing
with a clear colored wing.
They have a body,
Legs, arms,
and a heart
and they are also smart!

A flying bug,
He asks you not to
give him a tug.

The bug is just one of us,
He has feelings.
He can also be appealing
when he crawls up your leg.

You might feel a shiver,
You might tremble or quiver!

But no worries.
All you have to remember is...
That he is a black spotted thing
With a clear colored wing!

WAITING WAITING
BY SARAH K.

Waiting, waiting.

Tick tock, tick tock.

Almost summer.

I can not wait.

No more school or tests.

YES!!!!!!

School is **OUT**.

I feel so happy I can scream.

Now I am going to

California!

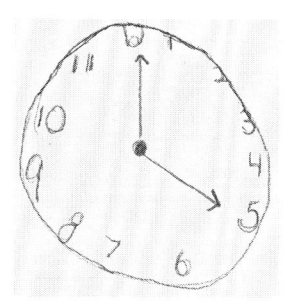

233   2009 © Nottingham Elementary School

My Incredible Imagination

MEANIE WEANIE
BY SUTTON C.

YOU'RE A MEANIE WEANIE
A MINI MEANIE WEANIE
MEANIE WEANIE
YOU SMELL LIKE FETTUCCINI
SO EAT YOUR FETTUCCINI YOU OH SO GRAND, MINI
MEANIE WEENIE.

YOU TASTE LIKE TORTELLINI
YOU LOOK LIKE BROCCOLINI
BUT SMELL LIKE FETTUCCINI
HOW COULD THIS BE YOU OH, SO GRAND, MINI MEANIE WEANIE?

YOU STOLE MY
    CHEF BOYARDINI.
NOW YOU SHALL BE A MEANIE WEANIE
WHO SMELLS LIKE
    FETTUCCINI
WHO TASTES LIKE
    TORTELLINI
AND LOOKS LIKE
    BROCCOLINI!!!!!

I LOVE YOU MEANIE WEANIE!!!!!!!

Tornado!
By Rick O.

Tornado!
Twisting with rage.
The strongest storm you'll ever see.
Take cover!
Or it won't be pleasant.
Tornado!
Twisting with rage.

BOOM!

By Ms. Ashley's Smarties 5

Poetry
By Jack Z.

I am fond of reading poetry,
But when I put poetry in writing
I don't feel free.

Writing poetry is hard.
I'd rather be in my backyard.
If I have to write 1100 poems
I will die,
Similar to a tuna fish on rye.

I'm not the next Emily Dickinson.
I'll probably be a Navy Seal.
(That's actually a job that's real.)
Besides, I normally just like to listen,

To poetry.

Whispering Wind
By Wil M.

I shoot like a brisk rocket,
I soar like a vibrant eagle,
Through the still, lifeless night

I glide through the air,
And swarm the bare trees

I whisper an eccentric song,
To the quiet animals lurking about

Their ears perk up,
And they come out of hiding,

To listen to,
My magical, majestic song

Chinchillas
By Kayla D.

Small and fluffy and good-natured
Feels like a soft stuffed animal
Silver mammals
Live in the high mountains of South America
Eats fruits, grains
Herbivores
Endangered
People use them for coats.
We can help
By not capturing the chinchilla.

My Incredible Imagination

A Colossal Milky Delight!
By Abby E.

Ch
  oc
    ol
      ate
        vanilla,
Banana split,
So many flavors,
So hard to pick!

Blueberry, strawberry,
Fruits are the best!
Say the word milkshake,
I'll say the rest.

Oreos, M&Ms,
Don't forget sweets!
Say any candy,
And shakes got 'em beat!

Swishy, swooshy,
A milky delight!
Adding some whipped cream
Is mighty – all right!

KA BANG KA BOOM!
By Allen A.

Ka bang ka boom
The colorful fireworks zoom,
Zooms a crazy
Sight to see a big rocket soars up and
Never ever comes down and with
A big boom
Loud explosions light up the sky

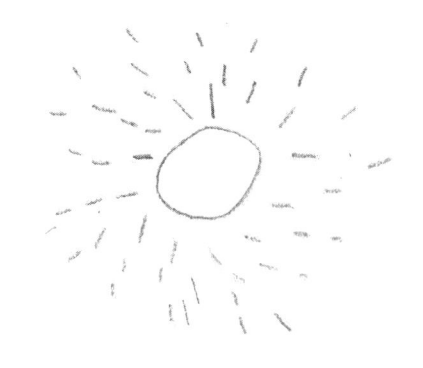

KA BANG KA BOOM!

By Mrs. Jones' Genius Gems   5

Snowy Day
by Alison P.

A light fluffy blanket

Covers the ground

As children run and

Stick out their tongues...

The snow is

Still falling.

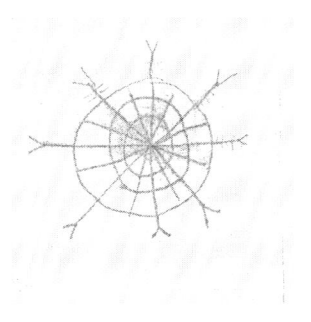

Once the children

Have had their fun

And the day is done…

The snow is

Still falling.

The never

Ceasing

Snow.

CHANGING CLOUDS
By Adelaide P.

Floating delicately in the sky, swoosh, swoosh,
Their lofty white twinkles by the blue.

Trickle, trickle, trickle,
The bright drops plummet
From the piercing gray shadow.

Thump, thump, thump,
The hail hits the ground.

The arcing rainbow connects the clouds.

My Incredible Imagination

All the Clocks
By Alec G.

The clock comes in various sizes,
Chattering, Clattering, Ticking, Tocking.
You see it in digital, alarm, grandfather, mantel,
Bracket, carriage, cuckoo, longcase, grandmother,
Black, brown, old fashion,
Numbers: 1, 2, 3, 4, 5, 6, 7, 8, 9, 10, 11, 12.

Textures smooth, maybe rough,
Very tall, sometimes small
Very hard, not soft,
Can be used in a loft.
Very ticking,
Very tock.
AM, PM, not DM!

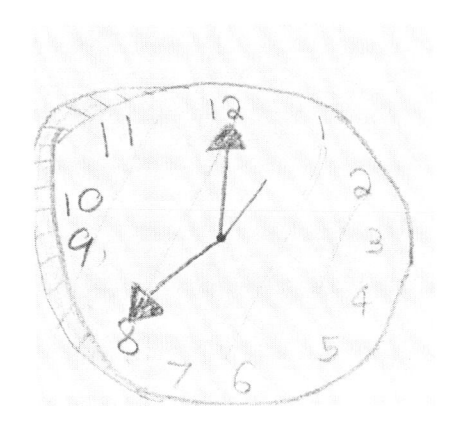

Bowling
By Nicholas S.

Avoid getting a zero, because they are not your hero. There is a foul line and if you cross it, your unhero comes. In most kinds of bowling, you should like a strike. Remember, you should be lucky to get any pins at all, one is better than none. There are many ways to bowl. One way is to curve the ball. Remember, not all curve the ball. Another way is to send the ball straight. That is great! In bowling, ball weights are between six and 16 pounds. Make sure that you do not use a ball that is too light or too heavy because your fate will not be too great. In America there are ten pins, in Europe, there are nine pins. But to me, more pins wins.

A wonderful sport, a tremendous sport indeed, a ball and some pins, that's all you need. Roll the ball 2X a frame 10 frames, that's a game.

By Mrs. Jones' Genius Gems 5

FAIRNESS
BY SAM H.

I once was nasty and cold hearted,
Then came a day blurred of how it started.

I got to school and no one cared.
I shoved over a chair and no one glared.

I called a kid names and no one sneered.
I capsized a desk and no one was feared.

After that day, I learned to be fair,
And if you're not, no on will care!!!

Water Fountain Snake
By Mackenzie F.

The curvy metal shines
A slick, silver fountain
With smooth snake eyes
Slyly slithering around
Slapping its eyes in its
Enemy's direction.
When the snake's first victim
Touches it slicks up
And shoots its sickening
Poison without sorrow
The snake's spooky water.

My Incredible Imagination

Snow Is Falling
By Suzanne D.

Snow, Snow, Snow,
   Falling and fluttering.
Snow, Snow, Snow,
   Topples and trips.
Snow, Snow, Snow,
   Drops and decreases.
Snow, Snow, Snow
   Declines and dives.
Snow, Snow, Snow,
   Sprinkles and splats,
Snow, Snow, Snow,
   Swings and swoops.
Snow, Snow, Snow.

Tornado
By Charlotte T.

Forever turning with wild whipping winds,
Animals running blind with fear,
Clouds of dust from the cracked Earth,
Dreading the return of the carousel of death.

By Mrs. Jones' Genius Gems 5

Slippery Snow Day
By Jack M.

Slipping and sliding all around,
  Snow sloshing up from the ground.

Sinking down in a garden of feathery snow,
  So many places on the ice to go.

Freezing but having lots of fun,
  Hoping there will be no sun.

Wind brushes across our frosty faces,
  Tripping and tumbling over untied shoelaces.

Creating snow angels, getting nice and wet,
  We've had lots of fun but we're not done yet.

We play non-stop on a world-wide ice rink.
  A happy virus spreads around the globe like a link.

A ticket out of school, that's the best part.
  This snow day is a masterpiece of art.

Books at Night
By Anna W.

During the day
Books sit books stay
Smack dab in the middle
Of my desk.

But at night I thought they
lay in their spot
But no much different from
that.

The fiction dance,
Fantasy read,
Historical on the computer,
Biography on a scooter.

The sun went up,
down the moon.
I came to school to find the
books in the fringes of the
room.

241 2009 © Nottingham Elementary School

My Incredible Imagination

FANTASTIC FRIENDSHIPS
By John L.

FRIENDSHIPS
AS FRAGILE AS GLASS.
YOU MAY HAVE FIGHTS
BUT JUST DON'T WORRY ABOUT
THE PAST. FRIENDS ARE AS
COMPLICATED
AS
A
RUBIX CUBE. SOME PROBLEMS WILL PASS LIKE WATER
THROUGH
A
TUBE.
THEY
MAY BE
NEIGHBORS   OR
FRIENDS   FROM
SCHOOL.   FRIENDS
ARE   LIFE'S
FAVORITE   TOOL.

Pencil
By Taylor O.

Scribble, scribble,
Write, write,
Black ink,
It sinks
Like skin,
Like skin.
It moves.
It dances,
Like a shadow,
Like a shadow,
On paper,
On gleaming white paper.

By Mrs. Jones' Genius Gems

Second Thoughts
By Eliza B.

red velvet
is what separates

me
and a world.
it rises
silky
slowly
swishy
too slowly

it makes me pause
and rethink
my decision
to throw myself
in this world

i glimpse it
for the first
magical
moment.

and all
my regrets
and second thoughts
are disregarded

and as i breathe in
ooooooh
and breathe out
ahhhhhhh
and immerse myself
in this theater
of a world.

My Incredible Imagination

Tiger
By Ben G.

The tiger stalks. It's deadly fast.
It waits around in the tall grass.
It sees a deer. It lunges back.
Its teeth are as sharp as a tack.
It pounces out and quickly, SMACK!
If you where here you'd probably sneer.
I bet you're glad you're not a deer.
The tiger eats its prided kill,
On top of a sunny hill.
Soon it slowly drifts to sleep.
Skin and bones lie in a heap.

My Wondorus mind
By: sarah O.

To me words are rain drops storming into my mind. My doctor said if I get too many ideas in my wondrous mind I might get a lot of pain and it's just to insane. But I think its kind of cool. Wait I think I caught a great idea in my mind. Let me find it for you. Oh shoot, I can't find it. Maybe next time Okay. Bye.

THE END!!!!

By Mrs. Jones' Genius Gems

Biography: V5
31 lines of funny poetry
By Christian M.

What do you know about Christian M.?
He's kinda good at baseball,
He sometimes talks some jive,
But his Little League batting average
Was a lowly .375.

But he had the highest on base percentage,
Due to all those four-ball walks,
And he was the most forceful guy,
'Cause he never shut the "talks."^

In football he's always there
For a catch when you need one.
He even caught one off of some defender's arm
While eating a hot dog and the bun^2.

He got an A in Social Studies,
And another one in Science.
And 2 more to go with them,
But a mortifying C in Writing^3.

He's got a feeling
He's not good at poetry,
But he does read a lot,
And he reads with a WPM rate of 103.

But in running he's really slow,
And to show that he had a 50-yd dash time of 10.0.

He's even won free burritos at the local Taco Bell,
And he's lost countless pencils; it's too many to tell!

But I'm afraid that's all I know
About that 10.91-year-old fellow.
So now I have to say goodbye…
…or to rhyme, Tally ho!
THE END

The Lies Revealed
^-The "talks" are me saying "Get a hit!" or "Get on base!" or "Were playing to win, people!"

^2- This statement is a hyperbole (pronounced hy-per-bo-lee), or a big lie, but the catch did happen. Alec passed to Sam, Victor tipped it, and I came running for the ball, caught in with one hand, and ran it for a touchdown to tie the game at 21, but I was NOT eating a hot dog.

^3- I really got a very low A-. (90.09%)

My Incredible Imagination

You're My Father
By: Bryn O.

Dedicated to my father,
whom I love with all my heart.

Through the sandy deserts,
Across the wonderful land,
You're my brilliant father who makes strong demands,
Sparkling and shining all day long,
You're my father who sings me songs.
You sleep at night, you also snore,
But you're my father who I'll love forever more.

The Sparkling Bonfire
By Alex R.

The ragging fire fights off the cold,

Rattling with light but filled with fumes.

Vivid with colors and shot with heat

A sleek performance made by he.

Hot with charcoal,

Killed by water.

Burning through wood and making ash.

By Mrs. Jones' Genius Gems

Lebray
By Emma T.

Letters conceal
    The entire page,
Making way for
    Illustrations,
When my mind
    Is parched I look
And gulp its
    Words one glance
Is all I need
    For each word is like
A cold refreshing
    Glass of lemonade
And each sentence
    Like a pitcher,
I cannot resist them
    Because to them
My mind is drawn.

Facts about existing elements attack
    And
Conquer my mind they make my
    Curiosity
Flee like a jack-rabbit dashing away
    From
An angered fox,
    They
Satisfy my questions for only a short
    While
For then like boiling water questions
    Bubble
Up again.

Let my imagination fly like a bird
    Let out of its cage,
My spirit suddenly alive like a
    Light-switch turned
    On,
The dragons and witches and magical
    Creatures are all
Brought to life,
    My mind is
        Free

Letters conceal
    The entire page,
Making way for
    Illustrations,
When my mind
    Is parched I look
And gulp its
    Words one glance
Is all I need
    For each word is like
A cold refreshing
    Glass of lemonade
And each sentence
    Like a pitcher,
I cannot resist them
    Because to them
My mind is drawn.

My Incredible Imagination

Orange
By Alden M.

Orange, Oh Orange, Really
Cool Yes
Oranges Are Really
Grand They Make Your Lips
Crumple.

Oranges Squish, Oranges
Squash
And Squirt When
You Consume Them.

Oranges Are Shrill When
They Strike The Ground.

Oranges Look Like A Splashing,
Jumping, Goldfish.

Oranges Make <u>Me</u> Joyful.

Evil Chairs
By Cecilia G.

Swivel ones,
Small ones,
Metal ones,
Plastic ones,
School ones,
Car ones,
And beach ones...
I've fallen off of each one,
Chairs simply do not like me,
Ever since I was a tot,
They make my legs and theirs,
Into a neat and simple knot!
EVIL!   OUCH!
EVIL!   OUCH!
EVIL!   OUCH!
FALL!   OUCH!
FALL!   OUCH!
FALL!   OUCH!

By Mr. Young's Einsteins

Brown Box
By Colleen C.

Brown, silent, stuffed in a closet, empty,
Boxes...
Just sitting there waiting...
So quiet I could hear a ghost whisper,
Waiting for what, well I mean boxes don't have anything to wait for...
Do they?

Just sitting there thinking...
In the dark of the night when nobody is there,
Thinking about what, well I mean boxes don't have brains...
Do they?

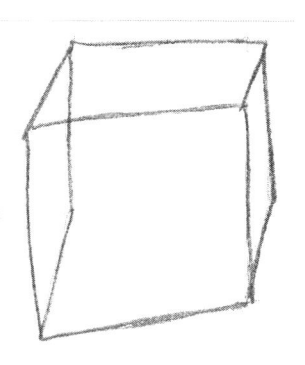

Wildfire
By Viktor G.

Crrrrrrrrrrrrrr pop
some dogwood burning
from a wildfire
the
color of a red apple
the smell of wood in
the winter the only
thing it does is kill
any thing in it's way
like a group of red horses

My Incredible Imagination

Words Are Like Peanut Butter
By Joanna S.

Peanut butter only tastes remarkable in a sandwich when it's with jelly
Words only sound remarkable when spoken with other words.

Peanut butter is brown, putting on a show in my mouth, on my taste buds
Words are all colors, putting on a show in your head, in your imagination.

Peanut butter sticks to your mouth like your legs stick to a chair on a hot summer day
Words stick to your mind like your tongue sticks to a metal spoon on a cold winter day.

Mix peanut butter before it can be enjoyed, like scoring the winning goal
Reflect on a word before it feels right, like winning first place in a swimming tournament.

Peanut butter is welcomed by mouths everywhere
Words are welcome to ears everywhere.

RODNEY DOES THE CAN-CAN
By Jonathan S.

Once in a brightly lit classroom,

"Can-can I-can-do-a can-can!" sang Rodney

"I can do-a can-can!" sang Bobby

"You-both-get DE-TEN-TION" yelped Miss Molly

"I-give-you PRE-VEN-TION" sang Principal Fred.

And they all lived happily ever after.

By Mr. Young's Einsteins   5

The Awful Chain
By Mark F.

It's the 6 foot chain
  You smell like disgusting rust
    You slither like a dull snake
      You sound like a dreary bell when you slither

You taste like a rotten onion
  You lie on the ship like a lazy king
    The chain
      The chain
        The chain, click, clack, ring............

Balloon Popper
By Maya L.

Just waiting...
Just floating in the air,
Just hanging there,
A light little circle,
That's all I am.

My life is done,
There's no where to go,
If someone could just untie me,
From this stubborn old pole,
Life would be a lot more fun!

Oh, here someone comes,
And they've got something with them...
It's kind of shiny...and pointy,
And it's thrusting right at me!
Wham-oh!

  POP!!!

Wow, I'm dead,
And my heart is broken,
Goodbye my friends,
As I lie in the open.

My Incredible Imagination

WIND
By Nora P.

I am the wind.
I float and drift around the world
I am the wind.
I am agile, a cool, quick flowing breeze
I am a soft comfort on a hot summer day
I am the wind.
I am a howling, angry bullet,
battering the cottages on the beach
I am the wind.
I am a bitter, freezing, hurling blizzard,
swirling snow in the air
I am the wind.
I am a crunching sound as I carry leaves off plants
on a colorful fall day
I am the wind.
I am a hurricane bending trees and
making huge waves
I am the wind.
I am a tornado, wrecking houses and
other structures
I am the wind.

Ice storm
By Matthew L.

The ice is falling
The branches are falling
The ice is making the crashing
Sound as it hits the ground
The ice stops falling
You go outside
You're falling to the ground on
The slippery ice.

By Mr. Young's Einsteins

Oh, Peculiar Walnutrus
By Sam B.

Oh, peculiar walnutrus, in summer you live up trees,
You lounge up there for three hot, long months, throwing seeds into the breeze.

These seeds crash in a stormy sea and walnutrus babies sprout!
Then they head to the island to swim their flippers out.

Some make it to the island; some make it to the trees,
They lounge up there for three hot, long months, throwing seeds into the breeze.

Morning Dove
By Reiss G.

```
   Chirp   flutter
   Chirp I flutter through the bright green trees,
         My white S
                   I
                     L
                   K
                       Y coat and my beautiful chirp,
     Let the world know that the morning has begun,
   The forest is now SURROUNDED with animals,
  Big, small, Q
           U      D they creep through the forest doing
           I      U their morning rounds, orange foxes
           E      O  with bleach white tails, catching
           T  and L   their juicy prey, voles, mice, squirrels, rabbits, are all hiding,
 blending in with the shadows of the trees,
   B   C   F   A    C
   L   A   I   N    R
   U   R   N   D    O
   E   D   C        W
       I   H       S,   are all gathering berries,
   B   N   E             oh, and me gently floating through the
   I   A   S,            trees, chirping, and singing the
   R   L                  beautiful song I
   D   S,
   S,                            SING!!!!
```

My Incredible Imagination

Line Breaks
By Sarah Jane R.

Why, oh why, do

        We have to s e p a r a t e   lines.....

How would   you feel

        if   you were *constantly s e p a r a t e d?*
With shapes, they are *sort of*
acceptable   but other than that, *I just don't know why!*

    All right fine, I will admit,   I adore line breaks a

        WEE bit!!! Line breaks give you a chance to imagine and I use them all
the time.
As you can see,
I am done sharing about my love for line breaks today. HOORAY!!!!

Snowy Snow
By Regan M.

Solid white and bright,
Snow is like vanilla ice cream.
Fluffy, and so silent and squashy,
Snow is so frosty,
But goes *crunch* when stepped on.

Piercing yells and screams!
Crazy crashes and smashes!
Sledding thrill,
Snow is a true delight!

By Mr. Young's Einsteins   5

Writer's Block
By Diana H.

I have writer's block in my head.
I lost my train of thought while sleeping in my bed.

I wish I could find something to write about
Like a pig with a stupendously big snout.

I feel like a falcon that missed its prey
'cause his brother was fooling while out to play.

I wish doctors had a pill to cure writer's block.
If they did, I wouldn't be looking at the clock.

I fell off my chair
and pulled out my hair because I had
writer's block!

Tick
Tock
Tick
Tock

AH HAAA!
I got an idea for the brain under my hair
By falling off my tangerine orange wheelie chair
YES!!!!!!!!!!!!!!!!!!!!!!!

The Tick Tock Clock
By Matthew S.

Slowly, slowly
The clock goes
Tick tock, tick tock.
It makes me dizzy so
I get up and go
In another room
Boom!!!
I fall on the floor
I get up and then fall on the floor again
Boom!!!

My Incredible Imagination

MIZZLE DRIZZLE
By Daniel D.

Drip drop
Drip drop
The sound
Of a downpour
Against a
Metal roof

Pitter Patter
Pitter Patter
Like the
Crash of
Words
Spilling onto
The script

Rain falling
From the sky
Occasionally
Fast like
Brain<u>storming</u>
At times *SLOOOW*
Reminiscent of
Final Draft

Pitter Patter
Pitter Patter
Awaiting it stops
Silence falls
Until tomorrow.

Cone of Doom
By Michael S.

The funnel comes down to attack the world, not to defend
There's a Tornado roaring, wet rain spurring Wind
Has come and laid to rest
Left behind its family
Crest of devastation
And mayhem
SILENCE

Another is coming its certainly is a spiraling doom
The winds have started a twin of the first
Then it darted over the field
Obliterating the house
Electrical wires
Boom boom
SILENCE

2009 © Nottingham Elementary School

By Mr. Young's Einsteins   5

Pie
By Denny H.

Pie is delicious,
Pie is round,
Pie is filled with food,
There are many types of pie such as……..
Meat pie, blueberry pie, apple pie, cherry pie, the most
Disgusting fish pie and many more.

Music
By Lexie L.

It's moving rhythm ringing

Carrying feeling to every note

As the sun rises, joyful music plays

When the moon peeks, lullabies are played

The soft, silvery sound attends the world

Music is something to enjoy

Pi
By Payton L.

What is pi, delicious?
No pi is
                    3.1415926538979

and much more
In fact pi goes on perpetually.
Why do people use pi?
    To find the distance around a circle (perimeter) formula pi x R 2